Macmillan/McGraw-Hill

Online Interactive Student Book

Texas Treasures

www.macmillanmh.com

LOG ON ▶ StudentWorks *Plus*
Interactive Student Book

VIEW IT 👁
- Preview weekly concepts and selections

READ IT 📖
- Word-by-Word Reading

LEARN IT 🖱
- Comprehension Questions
- Research and Media Activities

FIND OUT ▶
- Summaries and Glossary in other Languages

LOG ON ▶ **Online Activities**
www.macmillanmh.com

- **Interactive activities** and **animated lessons** for guided instruction and practice

IWB Interactive White Board Ready!

Texas Treasures

A Reading/Language Arts Program

Mc Graw Hill **Macmillan/McGraw-Hill**

Contributors

Time Magazine, Accelerated Reader

  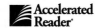

Students with print disabilities may be eligible to obtain an accessible, audio version of the pupil edition of this textbook. Please call Recording for the Blind & Dyslexic at 1-800-221-4792 for complete information.

B

The McGraw·Hill Companies

 Macmillan/McGraw-Hill

Published by Macmillan/McGraw-Hill, of McGraw-Hill Education, a division of The McGraw-Hill Companies, Inc., Two Penn Plaza, New York, New York 10121.

Printed in the United States of America

ISBN: 978-0-02-200024-0, Bk. 2
MHID: 0-02-200024-0, Bk. 2

6 7 8 9 DOW 13 12 11

Texas Treasures

A Reading/Language Arts Program

Program Authors

Diane August
Donald R. Bear
Janice A. Dole
Jana Echevarria
Douglas Fisher
David Francis
Vicki Gibson
Jan E. Hasbrouck
Scott G. Paris
Timothy Shanahan
Josefina V. Tinajero

 Macmillan/McGraw-Hill

Unit 4

Teamwork
Better Together

Award Winning Author

Award Winning Selection

iv

Science

Growing and Changing

The Big Question

THEME: A Plant's Life

THEME: Garden Plants

Show What You Know • REVIEW

Spotlight on Grade 2
The World Around Us

ix

2

The **Big** Question

How is working together better than working alone?

LOG ON ▶ VIEW IT

Theme Launcher Video
Better Together
www.macmillanmh.com

How is working together better than working alone?

Some jobs are too big for one person to do. Jobs are easier and done faster when we work with other people. Cleaning up the classroom takes a short time when everyone helps. Construction workers work in teams to build bridges, buildings, and roads. In this unit you will learn different ways people work together to complete big tasks. Learning about teamwork will help you work together with other people to get big projects done quickly.

Research Activities

Throughout the unit you will gather information about different places where teamwork happens. As a class we will make a list of topics and create open-ended questions. Then we will research one example from the list.

Keep Track of Ideas

Keep track of what you learn in the **Layered Book Foldable**. On the top flap, write "Better Together." On remaining flaps, write "Teamwork at home," "Teamwork at school," and "Teamwork at play." Write facts you learn about where teamwork happens.

Teamwork and Rules

When talking about Working Together with the class, it is important to agree on and follow rules.

- Listen to others.
- Raise your hand to speak.
- Ask questions and make comments when called on.

Discuss with the class other rules that are important to follow.

Digital Learning

LOG ON ▶ **FIND OUT** www.macmillanmh.com

 StudentWorks *Plus*

Interactive Student Book

- **Research Roadmap**
  Follow a step-by-step guide to complete your research project.

Texas Online Resources

- Topic Finder and Other Research Tools
- Videos and Virtual Field Trips
- Photos and Drawings for Presentations
- Related Articles and Web Resources
- Texas Web Site Links

All About TEXAS

Texas State Capitol
The Texas state capitol is located in Austin. It was completed in 1888. It is the nation's largest capitol.

5

6

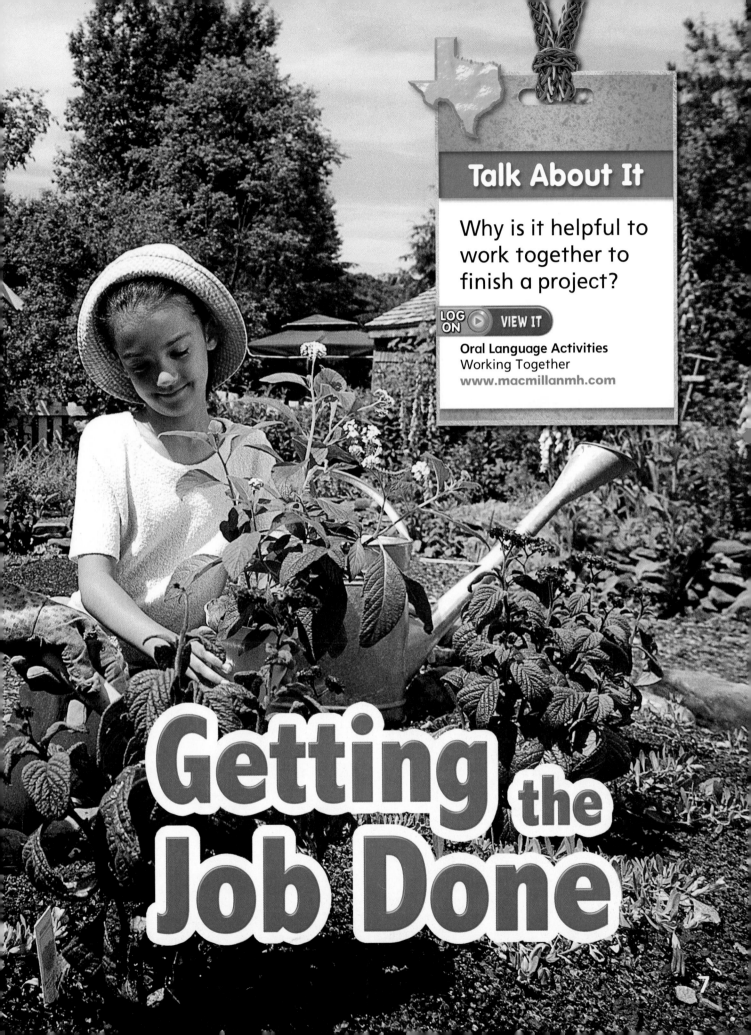

Talk About It

Why is it helpful to work together to finish a project?

LOG ON ▶ VIEW IT

Oral Language Activities
Working Together
www.macmillanmh.com

Getting the Job Done

TEKS Context Clues

To clarify information in stories, use context clues in sentences to help you figure out the meaning of an unfamiliar word.

When you breathe, you *take air into and out of your lungs.*

The Story of the Giant Carrot

by Rosa Manuel

One day Farmer Smith planted carrot seeds. The next morning he looked outside and **gasped**. He took a gulp of air because he was so surprised. A giant leaf was growing in the garden. He knew what would be **attached**. Giant leaves are joined to giant carrots!

Farmer Smith ran outside **frantically**. He was very, very excited. He jumped up and grabbed the leaf. It was so high, he **swung** from it! His body waved from side to side. Once his feet were back on the ground, he pulled on the leaf. The giant carrot would not come out.

First he called to his family for help. The family pulled, but the carrot was too big. Then he asked his neighbors to help. They pulled so hard that they had to stop to catch their breath. Finally he called to the dog and cow for help. They all pulled, and at last the carrot popped out!

The Smith family fed the whole town with the **delicious** carrot. Everyone said it was the best-tasting carrot they had ever eaten!

Reread for **Comprehension**

Cause	→	Effect

Reread

TEKS **Cause and Effect** A cause is why something happened. An effect is what happens. Rereading parts of a story can help you figure out the cause and effect in a story. Use the Cause and Effect chart to fill out information as you read.

LOG ON ▶ LEARN IT Comprehension
www.macmillanmh.com

Comprehension

Genre
A Folktale is usually a made-up story that takes place long ago.

Reread
TEKS Cause and Effect
As you read, use your Cause and Effect Chart.

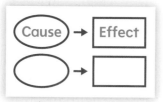

Read to Find Out
What causes the body parts to work together?

Head, Body, Legs

A Story From Liberia

retold by
Won-Ldy Paye & Margaret H. Lippert
illustrated by Julie Paschkis

Award Winning Author

Long ago, Head was all by himself.

He had no legs, no arms, no body. He rolled everywhere. All he could eat were things on the ground that he could reach with his tongue.

At night he rolled under a cherry tree. He fell asleep and dreamed of sweet cherries.

One morning Head woke up and thought, "I'm tired of grass and mushrooms. I wish I could reach those cherries."

He rolled himself up a little hill. "Maybe if I get a good head start I can hit the trunk hard enough to knock some cherries off," he thought. He shoved with his ears and began to roll down the hill. "Here I go!" he shouted.

Faster and faster he rolled.

CRASH!

"OWWWW!" he cried.

"Who's there?"
someone asked.

Head looked up.
Above him **swung**
two Arms he had
never seen before.

"Look down here,"
Head said, "and
you'll see."

"How can we look?"
asked Arms. "We don't
have eyes."

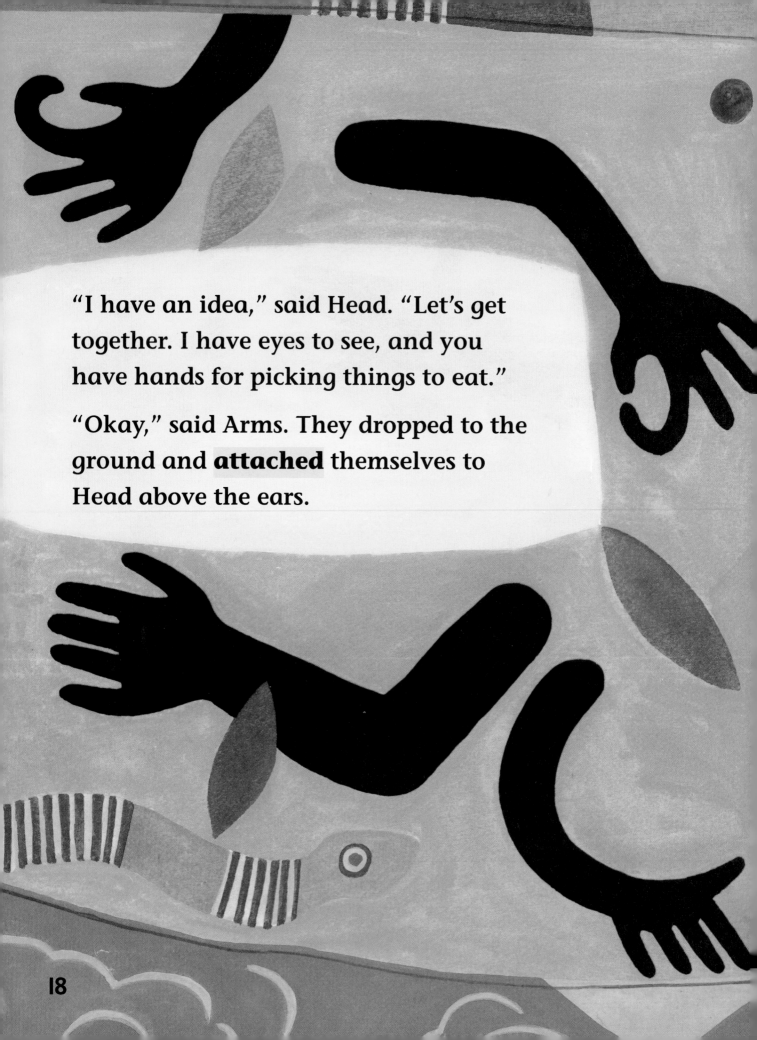

"I have an idea," said Head. "Let's get together. I have eyes to see, and you have hands for picking things to eat."

"Okay," said Arms. They dropped to the ground and **attached** themselves to Head above the ears.

18

"This," said Head, "is perfect."

19

Hands picked cherries, and Head ate every single one.

"It's time for a nap," said Head, yawning. Soon he was fast asleep.

While Head slept, Body bounced along
and landed on top of him.

"Help!" **gasped** Head. "I can't breathe!"
Arms pushed Body off.

"Hey," said Body. "Stop pushing me.
Who are you?"
"It's us, Head and Arms," said Head.
"You almost squashed us. Watch where
you're going!"

"How can I?" asked Body. "I can't see."

"Why don't you join us?" said Head. "I see some ripe mangoes across the river. If you help us swim over there, I'll help you see where you're going."

"Okay," said Body. So Head attached himself to Body at the belly button.

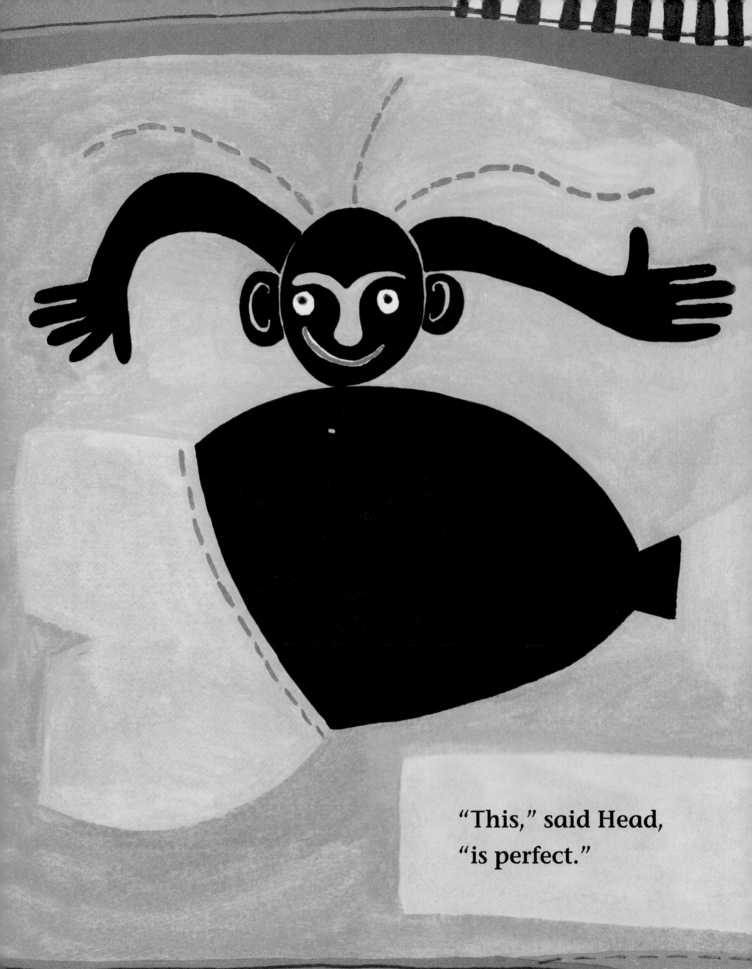

"This," said Head,
"is perfect."

They bounced down the bank into the river.

"Pull right . . . pull left," Head shouted to Arms, who paddled **frantically** against the current.

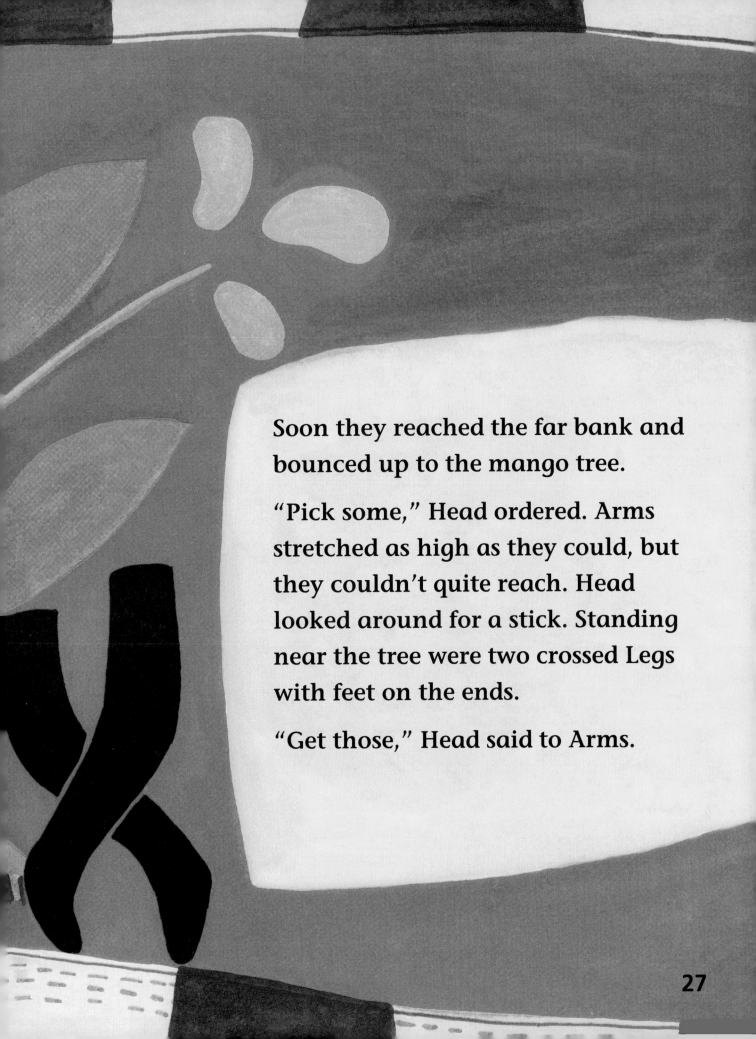

Soon they reached the far bank and bounced up to the mango tree.

"Pick some," Head ordered. Arms stretched as high as they could, but they couldn't quite reach. Head looked around for a stick. Standing near the tree were two crossed Legs with feet on the ends.

"Get those," Head said to Arms.

Arms grabbed them.
"Let us go!" shouted Legs.

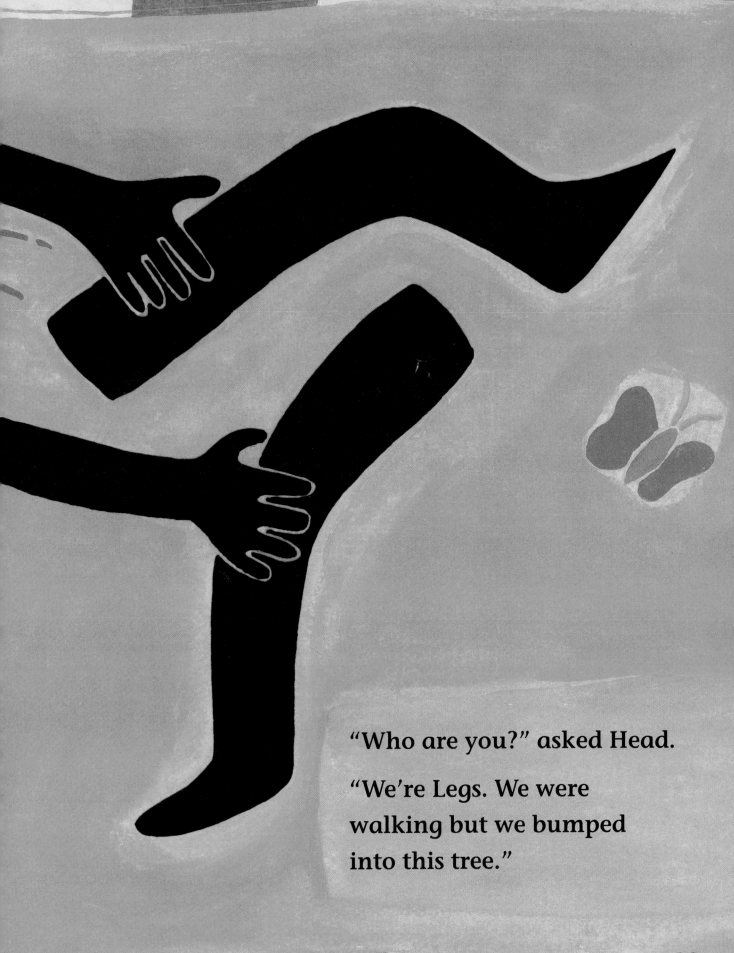

"Who are you?" asked Head.

"We're Legs. We were walking but we bumped into this tree."

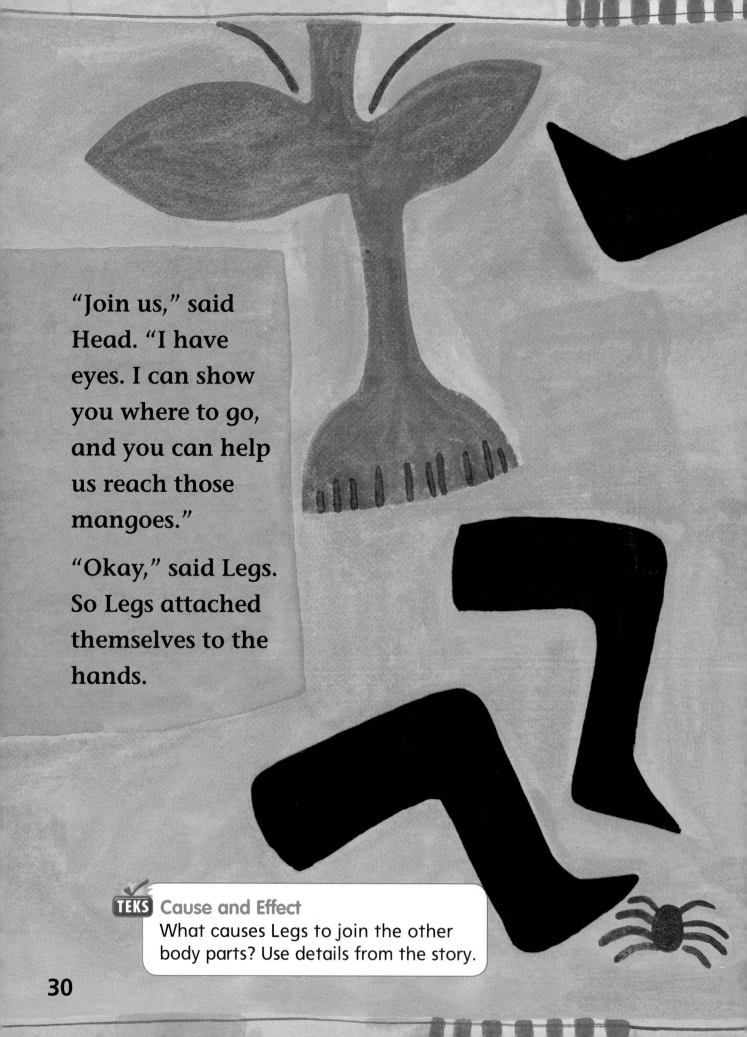

"Join us," said Head. "I have eyes. I can show you where to go, and you can help us reach those mangoes."

"Okay," said Legs. So Legs attached themselves to the hands.

TEKS **Cause and Effect**
What causes Legs to join the other body parts? Use details from the story.

"Not there," said Arms. "The hands need to be free to pick mangoes."

"I should be in the middle," said Body, "because I'm the biggest."

31

"That's right," said Head. "You should be at the bottom, Legs. I'll swing around on top of Body so I can see everything. And Arms, you move to the shoulders."

Everyone slid into place.
Legs stood on tiptoe. Body
straightened out. Arms
stretched up and the
hands picked a mango.
Head took a bite.

"Mmm, **delicious**," Head said.
"Now THIS is perfect!"

Telling stories with the Authors and Illustrator

Won-Ldy Paye came to this country from Liberia, which is in Africa. He is a storyteller as well as a writer. To write *Head, Body, Legs,* Won-Ldy worked with children's writer **Margaret Lippert**. Margaret travels all over the world learning folk stories. She shares her stories by writing children's books.

Artist **Julie Paschkis** is also a storyteller. She says she tells stories through her art. Julie has illustrated many children's books.

Another book by Won-Ldy Paye, Margaret Lippert, and Julia Paschkis

LOG ON ▶ FIND OUT

Authors Won-Ldy Paye and Margaret Lippert
Illustrator Julie Paschkis
www.macmillanmh.com

Author's Purpose

Won-Ldy Paye and Margaret Lippert worked together to tell a story. Think about a time you worked with others to do something. What did you do? Write about the experience.

TEKS Comprehension Check

Retell the Story

Use the Retelling Cards to retell the story.

Retelling Cards

Think and Compare

1. What does Head dream about?
   Details

2. What is the effect of all the body parts joining together? Use details from the story to help support your answer.
   Cause and Effect

3. How did Head, Body, and Legs feel when they were each alone? **Make Inferences**

4. Head, Body, and Legs worked together. What is the author's purpose for writing this story?
   Author's Purpose

5. How is *Head, Body, Legs* like "The Story of the Giant Carrot" on pages 8–9? **Reading/ Writing Across Texts**

Watch It Move!

Favorites \ History \ Search \ Scrapbook

Science

Genre

Expository An Internet article gives facts about a topic and is found on the World Wide Web.

 TEKS **Text Feature**

The **Drop-Down Menu** in an Internet article has links to related information on the Web site.

Content Vocabulary

force

friction

gravity

Rolling a ball and pulling a wagon are both examples of **force**. Force changes the way an object moves. Force can be a push, like when you roll a ball to a friend. Force can also be a pull, like when you drag a wagon.

Another force is called **friction**. Friction is when two things rub against each other. A ball slows down because of friction with the floor.

Gravity is a force, too. Hold a ball over your head and let it go. The ball will fall because Earth's **gravity** pulls it down.

Force and Motion Links

For more information about force and motion, check out:

- Experiments in Force and Motion

- The Force of Gravity

- Understanding Friction

TEKS Connect and Compare

1. What other information about force can you link to in this article? **Drop-Down Menus**

2. Think about this article and *Head, Body, Legs: A Story from Liberia.* What kind of force do the arms use to paddle across the river? **Reading/Writing Across Texts**

 Science Activity

Research force and motion activities online. Choose an activity and show it to the class. Explain why you chose this activity. Remember to speak at an appropriate pace.

LOG ON ▶ FIND OUT **Science** Force and motion
www.macmillanmh.com

Writing

TEKS **A Strong Paragraph**

A **strong paragraph** has a topic sentence and details that support it.

This is the topic sentence of my paragraph.

I include details that give more information about my topic.

Teamwork in the Park

Last month my whole class worked together to clean up the town playground. It was a big job. Pieces of paper and empty cans covered the ground. All 15 students worked as a team to throw away the garbage. It took more than four hours to get the job done. I am glad there were so many people to sweep and put trash in bags. Thanks to teamwork, the playground is now a clean and fun place for kids to play!

Your Writing Prompt

Some jobs are too big for one person to do alone.

Think about a time when you worked in a group or on a team to get something done.

Now write a personal narrative about that event.

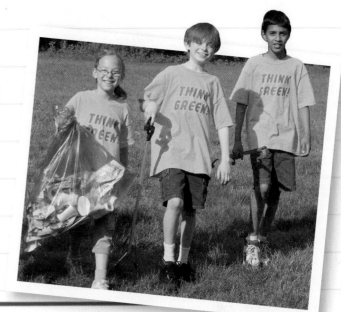

Writer's Checklist

✓ My writing clearly tells about a time when I worked in a group.

✓ My writing has a **strong paragraph** with a topic sentence and supporting details.

☑ The details in my writing give more information about the topic.

✓ I put capital letters and punctuation in the right places. I use linking verbs correctly.

Talk About It

Describe how working on a team is better than working alone.

Oral Language Activities
Special Teams
www.macmillanmh.com

SPECIAL TEAMS

Vocabulary

attention
buddy
accident
tip
enormous
obeys

TEKS Context Clues

Synonyms are words that have almost the same meaning.

Enormous and *huge* are synonyms.

SAFETY AT SCHOOL

by Brian Sullivan

"We need to talk about the school rules," our teacher, Mr. Wall, said. It was the second day of school. "What do you do when I turn out the lights?"

"Pay **attention** and listen carefully to you," said Pete.

"Good," said Mr. Wall. "What about lining up?"

"Find your line **buddy** and stand in line at the door," said Rosa.

"Right!" said Mr. Wall. "Remember, your line buddy is the friend you line up with. What is another rule, Julia?"

"No running in the halls," Julia said. "No one wants to fall or slip and have an **accident**."

"Good **tip**," said Mr. Wall. "That's helpful information to keep in mind. Also, why should we stay together in the halls?"

"This school is **enormous**. It's so huge it would be easy to get lost," said Liam.

"I know you all will follow the rules," said Mr. Wall. "When everyone **obeys** them, we stay safe."

Reread for **Comprehension**

Illustration	What I Learn From the Picture

Read Ahead

TEKS **Use Illustrations** Reading ahead and using illustrations can help you understand story events and give you some ideas about what might happen next. Use the chart to understand what the illustrations tell you about this story.

LOG ON ▶ LEARN IT Comprehension
www.macmillanmh.com

45

NEVER PLAY WITH MATCHES.

WASH YOUR HANDS AFTER YOU USE THE TOILET.

Comprehension

Genre
Fiction is a story with made-up characters and events.

TEKS **Read Ahead**

Use Illustrations

As you read and look at the pictures, use the Illustrations Chart.

Illustration	What I Learn From the Picture

Read to Find Out

How do the illustrations help make the story funny?

#16 NEVER PUT Your SOCKS in the MICROWAVE OVEN

#15 NEVER USE A BLOWDRYER in the BATHTUB

#74 STAND UP IN A BUS WHILE IT'S MOVING

#73 NEVER SIT TOO CLOSE TO THE T.V.

NEVER SIT TOO CLOSE TO THE TELEVISION.

NEVER EAT MAYONNAISE THAT'S BEEN SITTING IN THE SUN.

46

OFFICER BUCKLE AND GLORIA

**written and illustrated
by Peggy Rathmann**

Officer Buckle knew more safety **tips** than anyone else in Napville.

Every time he thought of a new one, he thumbtacked it to his bulletin board.

Safety Tip #77
NEVER stand on a SWIVEL CHAIR.

Officer Buckle shared his safety tips with the students at Napville School.

Nobody ever listened.

Sometimes, there was snoring.

Afterward, it was business as usual.

Mrs. Toppel, the principal, took down the welcome banner.

"NEVER stand on a SWIVEL CHAIR," said Officer Buckle, but Mrs. Toppel didn't hear him.

49

Then one day, Napville's police department
bought a police dog named Gloria.

When it was time for Officer Buckle to
give the safety speech at the school, Gloria
went along.

"Children, this is Gloria," announced
Officer Buckle. "Gloria **obeys** my
commands. Gloria, SIT!" And Gloria sat.

Officer Buckle gave Safety Tip Number One:

"KEEP your SHOELACES tied!"

The children sat up and stared.
Officer Buckle checked to see if Gloria
was sitting at **attention**. She was.

"Safety Tip Number Two," said
Officer Buckle.

**"ALWAYS wipe up spills BEFORE
someone SLIPS AND FALLS!"**

The children's eyes popped.
Officer Buckle checked on
Gloria again.
"Good dog," he said.

Officer Buckle thought of a safety tip he had discovered that morning.

"NEVER leave a THUMBTACK where you might SIT on it!"

The audience roared.

Officer Buckle grinned. He said the rest of the tips with *plenty* of expression.

The children clapped their hands and cheered. Some of them laughed until they cried.

Officer Buckle was surprised. He had never noticed how funny safety tips could be.

After *this* safety speech, there wasn't a single **accident**.

The next day, an **enormous** envelope
arrived at the police station. It was stuffed
with thank-you letters from the students at
Napville School.

Every letter had a drawing
of Gloria on it.

Officer Buckle thought
the drawings showed a lot
of imagination.

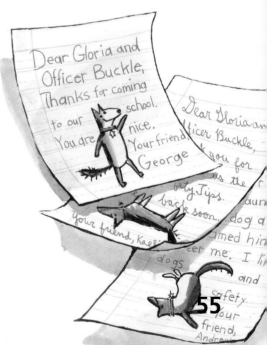

His favorite letter was written on a star-shaped piece of paper. It said:

You and Gloria make a good team.

Your friend,
Claire

P.S. I always wear a crash helmet.
(Safety Tip #7)

Officer Buckle was thumbtacking Claire's letter to his bulletin board when the phones started ringing. Grade schools, high schools, and day-care centers were calling about the safety speech.

"Officer Buckle," they said, "our students want to hear your safety tips! And please, bring along that police dog."

Officer Buckle told his safety tips to
313 schools. Everywhere he and Gloria went,
children sat up and listened.

After every speech, Officer Buckle took
Gloria out for ice cream.
Officer Buckle loved having a **buddy**.

Then one day, a television news team videotaped
Officer Buckle in the state college auditorium.
When he finished Safety Tip Number Ninety-nine,

**DO NOT GO SWIMMING DURING
ELECTRICAL STORMS!,**

the students jumped to their feet and applauded.

"Bravo! Bravo!" they cheered.
Officer Buckle bowed again and again.

That night, Officer Buckle watched himself on the 10 o'clock news.

 TEKS **Use Illustrations**
What does Officer Buckle find out about his safety speeches? Use the illustrations to explain your answer.

The next day, the principal of Napville School telephoned the police station.

"Good morning, Officer Buckle! It's time for our safety speech!"

Officer Buckle frowned.

"I'm not giving any more speeches! Nobody looks at me, anyway!"

"Oh," said Mrs. Toppel. "Well! How about Gloria? Could she come?"

Someone else from the police station gave Gloria a ride to the school.

Gloria sat onstage looking lonely. Then she fell asleep. So did the audience.

After Gloria left, Napville School had its biggest accident ever....

It started with a puddle of banana pudding....

SPLAT!
SPLATTER!
SPLOOSH!

Everyone slid smack into Mrs. Toppel,
who screamed and
let go of her hammer.

The next morning, a pile of letters arrived at the police station.

Every letter had a drawing of the accident.

Officer Buckle was shocked.

At the bottom of the pile was a note written on a paper star.

Officer Buckle smiled.

The note said:

Gloria missed you yesterday!

Your friend,
Claire

P.S. Don't worry, I was wearing my helmet! (Safety Tip #7)

Gloria gave Officer Buckle a big kiss on the nose. Officer Buckle gave Gloria a nice pat on the back. Then, Officer Buckle thought of his best safety tip yet...

Safety Tip #101

"ALWAYS STICK WITH YOUR BUDDY!"

A Good Laugh with Peggy Rathmann

Peggy Rathmann got the idea for *Officer Buckle and Gloria* from a videotape. The tape shows Peggy's mother talking. In the background, their dog licks the eggs that were set out for breakfast.

The next part of the tape, Peggy says, "shows the whole family at the breakfast table, complimenting my mother on the delicious eggs." Of course, no one knew what the dog had done! "The first time we watched that tape we were so shocked, we couldn't stop laughing," Peggy says.

Other books written by Peggy Rathmann

LOG ON ▶ **FIND OUT**

Author Peggy Rathmann
www.macmillanmh.com

Author's Purpose

Peggy Rathmann wrote this story to show what can happen in the background. Have you ever done something behind the scenes without anyone knowing it? What did you do?

TEKS Comprehension Check

Retell the Story

Use the Retelling Cards to retell the story.

Retelling Cards

Think and Compare

Illustration	What I Learn From the Picture

1. Where does Officer Buckle place his safety tips? Facts

2. What do the illustrations tell you about Gloria's personality? Illustrations

3. Why do the children start listening to Officer Buckle's safety tips? Make Inferences

4. What does the author want you to know about Officer Buckle and Gloria's friendship? Character

5. How are the safety tips in "Safety at School" on pages 44–45 different from Officer Buckle's tips? Reading/Writing Across Texts

71

Fire Safety

Social Studies

Genre
Expository text gives information about real people, things, or events.

TEKS Text Features
Floor Plans are maps that show where all the rooms in a building are.

Content Vocabulary
hazards

route

calm

Firefighters want everyone to be safe. They teach families how to avoid fire **hazards**, which are dangerous items or situations. You can help prevent fires by following fire safety rules. You can also stay safe by knowing what to do if a fire starts nearby.

How to Stay Safe from Fire

- Never play with matches or lighters.

- Do not touch lit candles.

- Do not cook unless an adult is with you.

- Be careful around irons, stoves, fireplaces, and grills.

- Never touch electric cords, plugs, or outlets.

Stop! Drop! Roll!

If your clothes catch fire, do these three things right away.

1

Stop! Running and walking can make fire worse.

2

Drop! Get down on the ground. Cover your face and eyes.

3

Roll! Roll over and over until the flames are out.

Make a Plan!

You and your family can learn how to stay safe if there is a fire in your home. Make a floor plan of your home. Mark the best ways to get out of the house. Make sure your plan has more than one **route** in case one path gets blocked. Pick a safe place to meet outside. Have fire drills to practice your plan. Practicing will help you stay **calm** and find a safe path to the outside.

Fire Safety Floor Plan

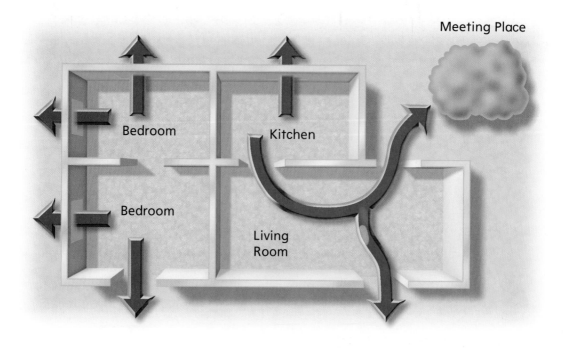

Meeting Place

Bedroom

Kitchen

Bedroom

Living Room

This floor plan shows several ways to get out of a home in case a fire starts.

After you are safely out of the house, call 9-1-1 for help. Wait for the firefighters to arrive. Never go back into the house for anything!

 ## Connect and Compare

1. What two escape routes from each bedroom does the floor plan show? **Floor Plan**

2. Think about this article and *Officer Buckle and Gloria*. What are some other safety tips that firefighters might try to teach to students and families? **Reading/Writing Across Texts**

Social Studies

Draw a floor plan of your home. Show two escape routes and an outside meeting place. Give a copy to your family. Then practice telling a family member the three steps you would take if your clothes caught fire. Be sure to tell the steps in order.

LOG ON ▶ FIND OUT **Social Studies** Fire safety
www.macmillanmh.com

Writing

TEKS A Strong Opening

Good writers create **strong openings** that interest their readers.

I wrote a strong opening sentence that tells about my essay topic.

My opening has a description.

Wear Your Bike Helmet

by Jay F.

I love riding my bike really fast, but I have learned how to be safe. Wearing a bike helmet every time you ride is important. Just last week I fell off my bike. But when my head hit the street, my helmet protected it. What would have happened if I hadn't worn my helmet? I hate to think about it! My helmet keeps me from getting really hurt. So be safe! Wear your bike helmet each time you ride!

Your Writing Prompt

Safety is very important.

Think about something you do that helps you stay safe.

Write an essay about how people can stay safe.

Writer's Checklist

✓ My essay is clearly about something people can do to stay safe.

☑ I include a **strong opening** to interest readers.

✓ I include important details that illustrate why safety is important.

✓ I use helping verbs correctly. All my sentences end with a punctuation mark.

Talk About It

Describe some jobs that groups of people need to work together.

 VIEW IT

Oral Language Activities
Worker Teams
www.macmillanmh.com

Worker Teams

TEKS

Vocabulary

serious

personal

aid

informs

heal

Paramedics come when someone is sick or hurt.

A Ride to Help

The lights flash and the sirens scream. An ambulance is on its way. There is a **serious** problem. Someone is hurt or very sick. It could be severe.

Paramedics drive the ambulance. They also give help to people on the way to the hospital. Inside the ambulance are medical supplies. If someone has a broken bone, the paramedics use special tools to keep it still.

Paramedics take a **personal** interest in helping people. They give **aid** and get people to the hospital as quickly as possible.

Time for an X-Ray

Who needs an X-ray? People who have broken a bone will usually get an X-ray taken at the hospital. An X-ray is a special kind of photograph that shows bones and other parts inside the body.

What happens when you get an X-ray? First an X-ray worker takes the picture. Then a doctor looks at the X-ray to find out if a bone is broken. Finally the doctor **informs** the patient about how the bone will **heal**. She may tell the patient that he or she needs a cast. The doctor also explains that the bone will mend over time.

A Trip to the Emergency Room

Who works in the emergency room?

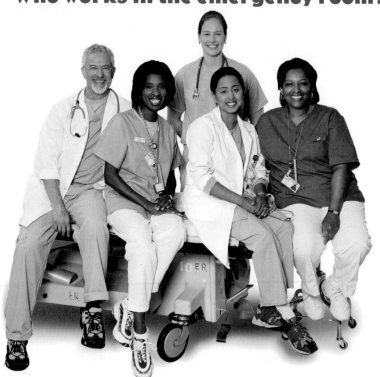

Oh, no! You have a broken bone. Where do you go? To the hospital emergency room, of course. The emergency room can be a busy place. Ambulances and people arrive there during the day and night. People are brought there if they have a **serious** medical problem.

Doctors and nurses work in the emergency room. Their job is to **aid** people who are sick or hurt. Other people help patients, too. They help keep the hospital running properly. Let's meet some of the people who work in a hospital emergency room.

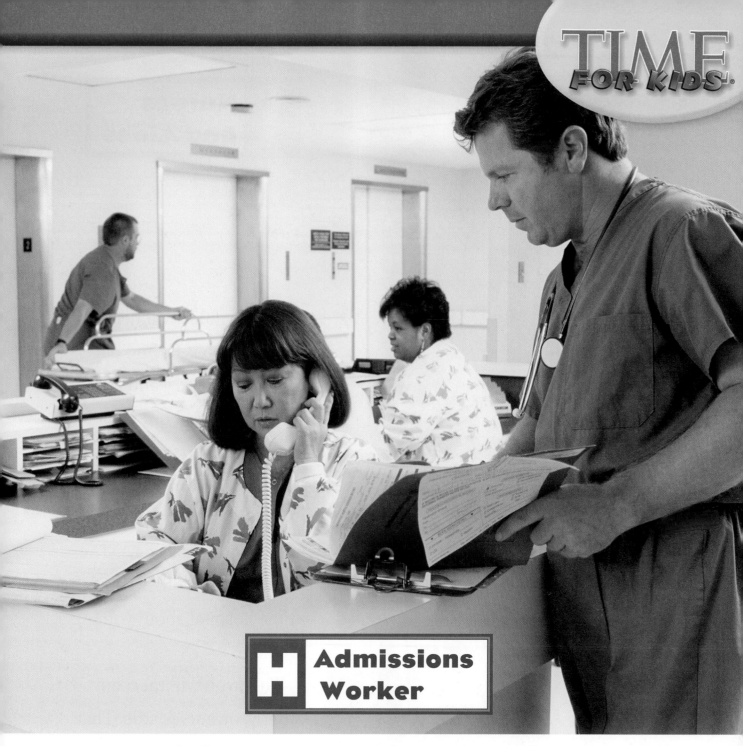

H Admissions Worker

The first person you see in the emergency room is an admissions worker. The hospital needs to keep track of the patients coming into the emergency room. The admissions person checks you in. The adult who is with you will fill out hospital forms. The forms ask for your **personal** information and why you came to the hospital.

Next a nurse will help you. A nurse's job is to find out about your injury and ask you questions about your health. The nurse will take your temperature and blood pressure and record this information on a chart. The nurse **informs** other people in the hospital about your problem.

Then you will meet an orderly, or nurse's aide. That person will help you get around in the hospital. She will take you to the correct department if you need to get tests done. She may use a wheelchair to take you from one area to another.

Doctor

Last, it's time for the doctor to examine you. The doctor checks your injury. He also looks at your chart. He arranges for you to get an X ray if you need one. The doctor knows how to fix your broken bone. He will probably put on a cast so the bone will **heal**. The doctor also decides whether you need to stay in the hospital or if you can go home right away.

So don't worry if you need to go to the emergency room. Now you know about the people who work there and how they will help you feel better.

TEKS Think and Compare

1. When do you go to the emergency room?

2. Describe the people you see in an emergency room in the order you meet them.

3. What would happen if the emergency room did not have an admissions worker?

4. How are paramedics similar to doctors? How are they different?

A Visit to the Dentist

1. **Y**ou need your teeth to eat. To take good care of them, eat healthful foods and remember to brush and floss every day. It's also important to visit the dentist every six months.

2. Here's what happens at a dental checkup. First the dentist takes X rays. These pictures of your teeth show if you have any cavities. They also show the health of your teeth and gums. Next the dentist or an assistant cleans your teeth and makes them shine.

3. Last, the dentist looks carefully inside your mouth. He or she uses a little mirror to see the teeth in the back of your mouth. The dentist is pleased when your teeth and gums are healthy! In six months it will be time to come back for another checkup.

DIRECTIONS
Decide which is the best answer to each question.

1 Look at the web of information below.

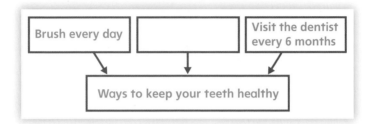

| Brush every day | | Visit the dentist every 6 months |

Ways to keep your teeth healthy

Which information from paragraph 1 belongs in the empty box?

(A) Look in your mouth

(B) Eat healthful foods

(C) Chew your food carefully

(D) Floss once a month

2 Why should you visit the dentist?

(F) To brush and floss

(G) To get shiny gums

(H) To check for cavities

(J) To see your teeth

3 This article was most likely written to —

(A) tell why you have teeth

(B) teach you how to brush well

(C) explain what dentists do

(D) show how x-rays work

Write to a Prompt

Pat wrote about a librarian who helped him.

I put the events in order to organize my writing.

Help at the Library

I went to the library last summer. There were so many books! I asked the librarian for help.

First, Ms. Valdez asked me what I liked to read. I said I liked both made-up stories and true stories. Next, Ms. Valdez helped me find two good books. One was fiction, about a talking cat. The other book was nonfiction. It was about a paramedic.

Last, I took the books home. They were both fun to read. Now I always ask Ms. Valdez for help at the library. She really knows how to find the right books for me.

Writing Prompt

Respond in writing to the prompt below. Review the hints below before and after you write.

Write about a time when someone helped you.

Writing Hints

☑ Remember to write about a time someone helped you.

☑ Plan your writing by organizing your ideas.

☑ Include important details to support your ideas.

☑ Check that each sentence helps the reader understand your writing.

☑ Use correct spelling, capitalization, punctuation, grammar, and sentences.

☑ Review and edit your writing.

COMMUNiTY TEAMS

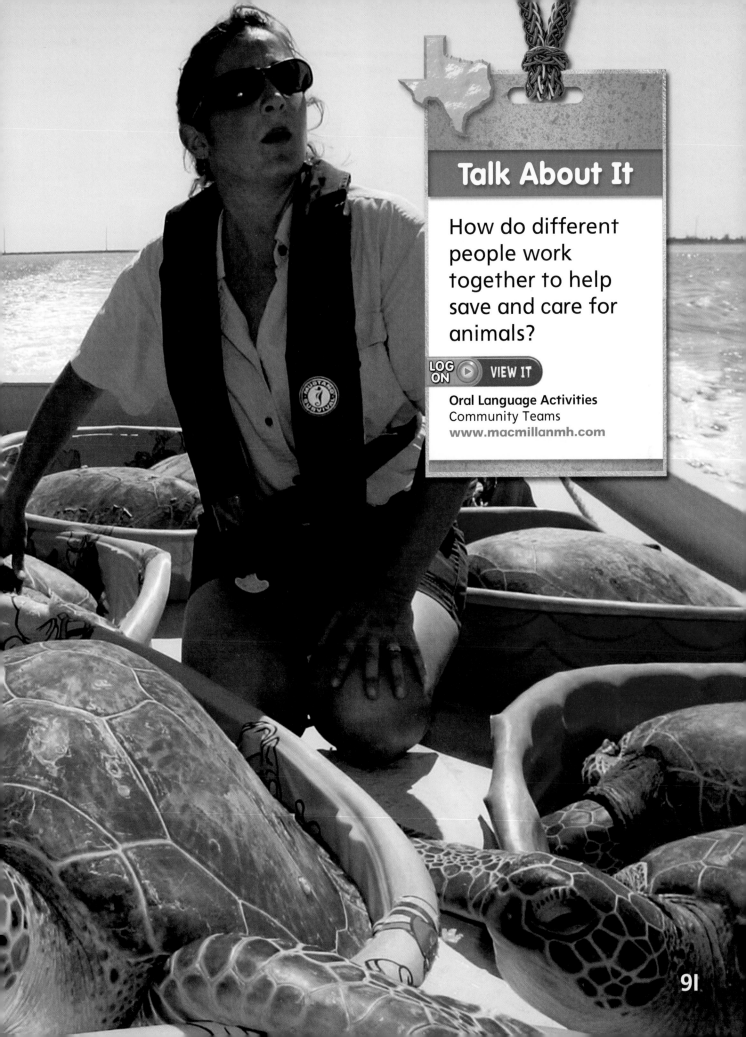

Talk About It

How do different people work together to help save and care for animals?

LOG ON ▶ VIEW IT

Oral Language Activities
Community Teams
www.macmillanmh.com

91

Vocabulary

| young |
| examines |
| mammal |
| normal |
| hunger |
| rescued |

TEKS **Context Clues**

Antonyms are words that have opposite meanings.

Young and *old* are antonyms.

Multisyllabic Words When reading multisyllabic words with single letters, remember to divide the word into syllables. Then decode each syllable.

A WHALE IS SAVED!

by Elizabeth Baker

A **young** whale got stuck in Drew Harbor today. The whale was small and had been born recently. Some people saw the whale in trouble. They called the police.

Soon help was on the way. Jenny Litz arrived first. She is a scientist who **examines** whales.

Jenny looks at every part of an animal to see if it is healthy. A whale is a **mammal**. Mammals are warm-blooded animals that have hair and drink their mother's milk. Jenny checked the whale's heartbeat and breathing. She said the whale seemed **normal**. There were no signs of illness.

Next Jenny checked to see if **hunger** was a problem. Going a long time without food can be dangerous for a whale. But this whale seemed healthy and well fed.

The helpers acted fast. They kept the animal wet. The tide slowly came in. The water got deeper. Soon the whale could swim again. At last the whale was **rescued**! Jenny and the other helpers saved the whale's life.

Reread for **Comprehension**

Analyze Text Structure

TEKS **Sequence of Events** Looking at how ideas and information are organized in a text helps to describe the sequence of events. Reread the article and use the chart to help you understand what happens first, next, and last to save the whale.

First

↓

Next

↓

Last

LOG ON ▶ LEARN IT Comprehension
www.macmillanmh.com

Comprehension

Genre
Expository text can be a retelling of a true event.

Analyze Text Structure

Sequence of Events
As you read, use your Sequence Chart.

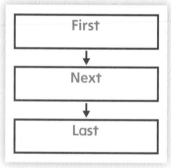

Read to Find Out
How is Sidney found, helped, and released to her ocean home?

94

A Harbor Seal Pup Grows Up

by Joan Hewett

photographs by Richard Hewett

By the Ocean

The harbor seal pup is 2 weeks old. Her name is Sidney. Sidney stays close to her mother. She drinks her mother's milk.

Waves crash on the rocky beach. Harbor seal families lie in the warm sun.

Sidney and her mother lie in the sun too.

Sidney's mother gets hungry. She dives in the water to catch fish. The water is too cold for Sidney. So Sidney stays on the shore.

The seal pup waits for her mother. She waits for 3 days. She is very hungry.

People notice the seal pup. She is alone. Will her mother come back?

The next day, the pup is still alone. The people call for help. Sidney is **rescued**.

 TEKS **Sequence of Events**

Think about what has happened so far. Use details from the text to describe how Sidney ends up alone on the beach.

Nursed Back to Health

Sidney is brought to a sea **mammal** center.

A scientist named Peter is in charge. Peter takes care of **young** seals. He lifts the thin pup from her cage.

Sidney is weak from **hunger**. Peter knows just what to do. He puts a tube in Sidney's mouth.

Then Nicole pumps a drink into Sidney's stomach. The drink is like a mother seal's milk.

Sidney is full. She is also very tired.
She falls asleep.

When Sidney wakes up, her eyes are bright. She looks around.

Peter **examines** the pup. Her heartbeat is **normal**. So is her temperature. She is healthy.

Sidney has a full set of teeth. That means she is at least 3 weeks old. Sidney is small for her age.

Sidney gets her drink 3 times a day. She becomes stronger. Using her flippers, she scoots around.

A child's plastic pool becomes Sidney's playpen. She likes the water. She swims faster and faster.

Nicole shows Sidney a fish. Sidney does not want it.

Nicole does not give up. Day after day,
she wiggles a fish in front of Sidney.
Then one day, the pup swallows it.

Before long, Sidney wants to eat fish. She waits for her bucket of fish in the morning.

The pup is gaining weight. She no longer needs her healthy drink.

Sidney is 5 weeks old. She has a thick layer of fat. The fat will keep her warm in cold water.

Sidney is ready to be on her own.

 TEKS **Sequence of Events**
Describe the order of events that people take to help Sidney at the sea mammal center.

Returning to the Ocean

Peter puts the pup in a carrying case. Other
scientists take over. They carry Sidney onto
a boat. Sidney is excited by the ocean's salty
smell. She shakes the case.

The boat heads toward an island. When they are almost there, the boat stops. It is time to say good-bye.

A scientist tips the case. "Good luck, little one," she says.

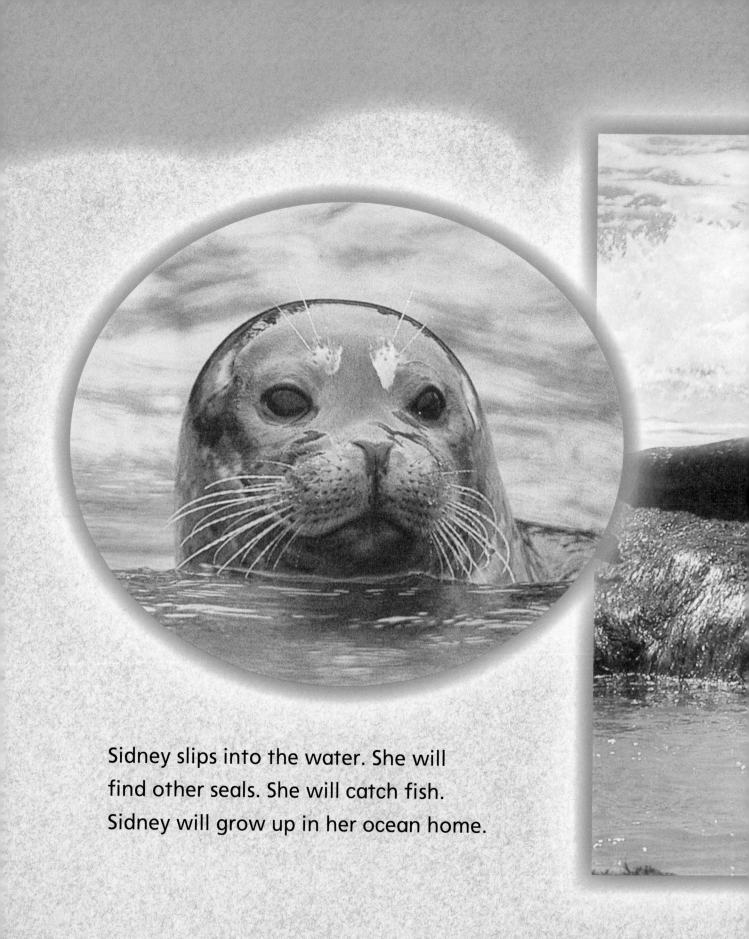

Sidney slips into the water. She will
find other seals. She will catch fish.
Sidney will grow up in her ocean home.

Joan and Richard Hewett's Animal Adventures

Joan Hewett and her husband, **Richard Hewett**, created their first children's book in 1977. After that, Richard says, "I knew that this was what I wanted to do. Children's books are the best."

Joan and Richard have worked on more than 20 children's books together. Many of these books are about animals. Joan says, "We always enjoy doing books that bring us in close contact with animals. Still, photographing harbor seals and other wild animals takes patience. It's a challenge, and that's part of the fun."

Other books by Joan Hewett and Richard Hewett

Authors Joan Hewett and Richard Hewett
www.macmillanmh.com

TEKS **Author's Purpose**

The Hewetts like to write about animals. Think about when you helped an animal or a person. Write a paragraph about how you helped.

TEKS Comprehension Check

Retell the Selection

Use the Retelling Cards to retell the selection.

Retelling Cards

Think and Compare

1. Where is Sidney taken to when she is **rescued**? Details

2. Use details to explain what happened to Sidney. Describe what happened first, next, and last. Sequence of Events

3. How do Peter and Nicole feel about Sidney? Make Inferences

4. Why does the author write about Sidney's time in the mammal center? Author's Purpose

5. How is Sidney like the whale in "A Whale Is Saved!" on pages 92–93? Reading/Writing Across Texts

First
↓
Next
↓
Last

115

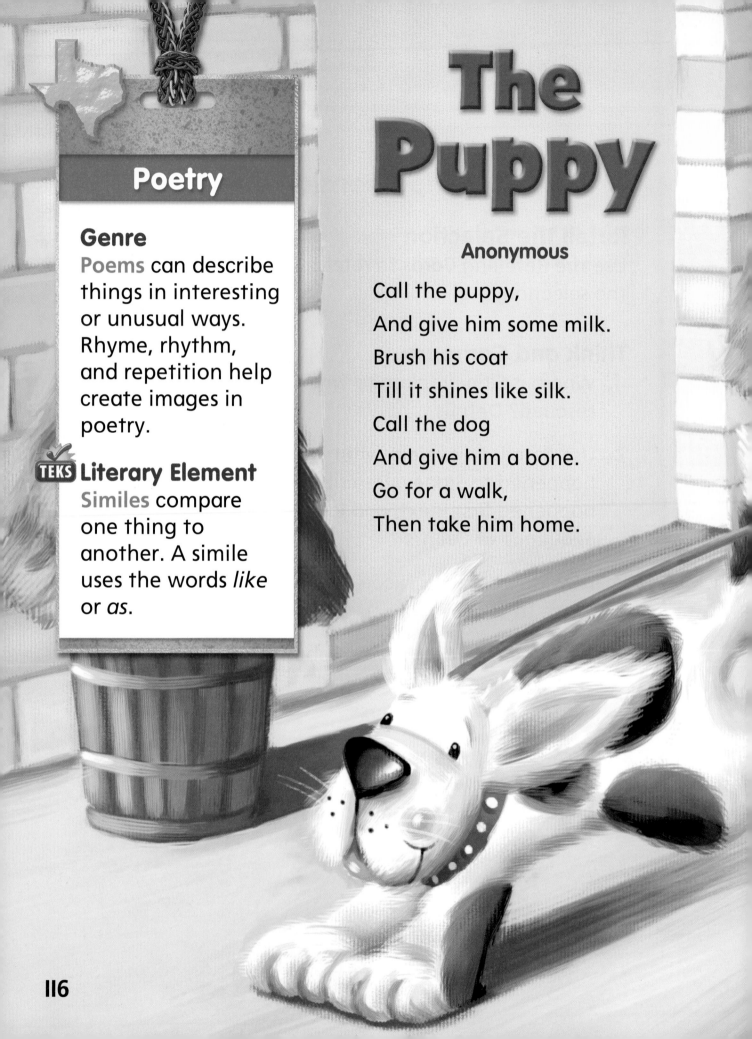

Poetry

Genre
Poems can describe things in interesting or unusual ways. Rhyme, rhythm, and repetition help create images in poetry.

TEKS Literary Element
Similes compare one thing to another. A simile uses the words *like* or *as*.

The Puppy

Anonymous

Call the puppy,
And give him some milk.
Brush his coat
Till it shines like silk.
Call the dog
And give him a bone.
Go for a walk,
Then take him home.

TEKS Connect and Compare

1. What things are compared in the poem? How can you tell that the comparison is a simile? **Simile**

2. Think about how the scientists cared for Sidney in *A Harbor Seal Pup Grows Up*. How is caring for a seal pup like caring for a puppy? How is it different? **Reading/Writing Across Texts**

LOG ON ▶ FIND OUT **Poetry** Animal care
www.macmillanmh.com

Writing

TEKS Important Details

Good writers use **important details** to make information in their writing clear to readers.

I give important details about Fred's water.

This detail tells how often to brush Fred.

Reading and Writing Connection

March 2, 2---

Dear Talia,

Thank you for taking care of my cat Fred while I am away. Taking care of Fred is easy! Starting tomorrow, give Fred two small cans of food each day. We already gave him food today. Fred needs a bowl of fresh water each morning, too. Please brush Fred's fur every two days. Fred needs lots of love so give him plenty of hugs.

Thanks for your help.

Sincerely,
Kim

Your Writing Prompt

An animal you take care of could be your pet or the pet of someone you know.

Think about what you need to do to care for this animal.

Write a letter to a friend that tells how to take care of this pet.

Writer's Checklist

✓ My writing is about how to care for an animal.

✓ My letter is organized to describe events in the correct order.

☑ I include important details that make the information in my letter clear to readers.

✓ I begin each new sentence with a capital letter. I use irregular verbs correctly.

Surprising Teamwork

Talk About It

When have you seen people work together in a surprising or an unusual way?

Vocabulary

menu
fetch
simmered
assembled
devoured

TEKS **Word Parts**

Verbs are action words that can have **word endings** like *-s*, *-ed*, or *-ing*. These endings tell you when an action took place.

The *-ed* ending means that the action happened in the past.

Yesterday we *devoured* the food.

Bobo's celebration

by Keith Fish

Mom and I planned a surprise party for my brother Bobo.

First, my mom and I made a **menu**. It listed all the foods we would serve. The main dish was Bobo's favorite—seaweed stew!

Mom asked me to **fetch** the things we needed, so I swam to the Ship Shop. When I went to pay, I knew that I was forgetting something. I checked my list. I had not remembered the seaweed! So I asked Ron Ray if he had any.

"Yes, I have some seaweed," he said. "That's 20 sand dollars, please." I paid him and swam home.

The day of the party, the stew **simmered** on the stove. I watched it bubble over low heat for hours.

An hour before the party, the guests **assembled** in one spot. The group gathered with Mom and me by the reef. When Bobo came, we yelled "Surprise!"

Bobo's party was fun. We **devoured** all of the stew. We ate until there was nothing left. Bobo said it was the best surprise ever!

Reread for **Comprehension**

Story Structure

TEKS **Fantasy and Reality** A fantasy story could not happen in real life. A reality story could happen. Reread the story and use details to fill in the chart. Based on the details, could "Bobo's Celebration" happen in real life?

Reality	Fantasy
What Could Happen?	What Could Not Happen?

LOG ON ▶ LEARN IT Comprehension
www.macmillanmh.com

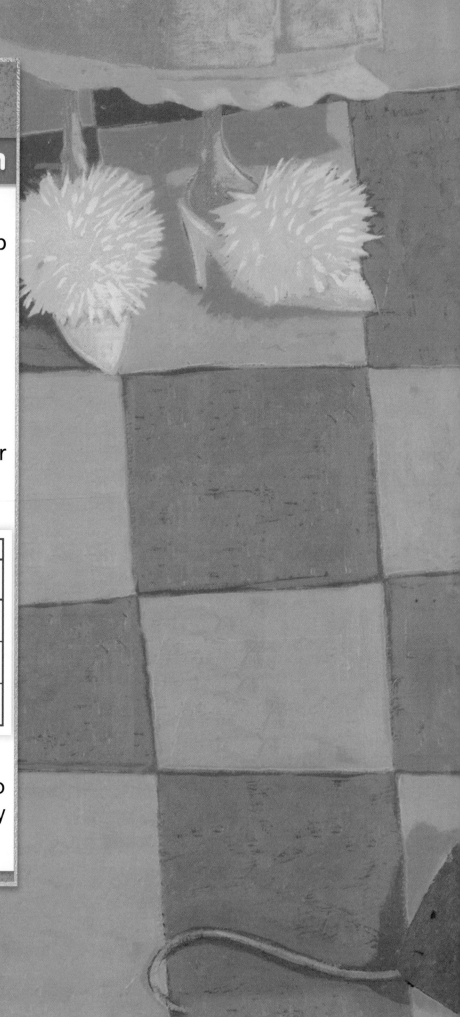

Genre
Fantasy has made-up characters, settings, or events that could not happen in real life.

Story Structure
TEKS **Fantasy and Reality**
As you read, use your Fantasy and Reality Chart.

Reality	Fantasy
What Could Happen?	What Could Not Happen?

Read to Find Out
What do the mice do in this story that they can't do in real life?

Award
Winning
Author

Mice
and
Beans

by Pam Muñoz Ryan

illustrated by
Joe Cepeda

Rosa María lived in a tiny house with a tiny yard. But she had a big heart, a big family, and more than anything, she loved to cook big meals for them.

In one week, her youngest grandchild, Little Catalina, would be seven years old, and the whole family would squeeze into her *casita* for the party.

Rosa María didn't mind because she believed what her mother had always said: "When there's room in the heart, there's room in the house, **except** for a mouse."

Sunday, Rosa María planned the **menu:** *enchiladas*, rice and beans (no dinner was complete without rice and beans!), birthday cake, lemonade, and a *piñata* filled with candy.

She ordered the birthday present—something Little Catalina had wanted for a long time.

Satisfied with the plans, she wiped down the table so she wouldn't get mice and took out a mousetrap just in case. She was sure she had set one the night before, but now she couldn't find it. Maybe she'd forgotten.

When it was set and ready to **snap,** she turned off the light and went to bed.

Monday, Rosa María did the laundry. She washed and ironed her largest tablecloth and the twenty-four napkins that matched. But when she finished, she only counted twenty-three.

"*No importa,*" she said. "It doesn't matter. So what if someone has a napkin that doesn't match? The important thing is that we're all together."

After dinner she swept the floor and checked the mousetrap.

But it was missing.

Didn't I set one last night? she wondered.

She hurried to the cupboard to **fetch** another, and when it was set and ready to **snap,** she turned off the light and went to bed.

Tuesday, Rosa María walked to the market. She filled her big *bolsa* with *tortillas,* cheese, red sauce, white rice, pinto beans, and a bag of candy. She bought a *piñata* and on her way home she stopped at the *pastelería* to order the cake.

After dinner, she washed the dishes and checked the mousetrap.

But it had vanished.

"*¡Qué boba soy!* Silly me, I must have forgotten, again!"

She hurried to the cupboard to fetch another and when it was set and ready to **snap,** she turned off the light and went to bed.

TEKS Fantasy and Reality
What illustrations so far tell you that this story might be a fantasy?

Wednesday, Rosa María prepared the *enchiladas*. She noticed the *piñata* was missing a few feathers.

"*No importa*," she said. "Those feathers won't make a difference to the children when the *piñata* is filled with candy."

After dinner she mopped up the sauce and checked the mousetrap. **But it was gone again!**

"I am so busy that I'm forgetting to remember!" she cried.

She hurried to the cupboard to fetch another and when it was set and ready to **snap,** she turned off the light and went to bed.

Thursday, Rosa María **simmered** the beans. She searched for her favorite wooden spoon, the one she always used to cook *frijoles,* but she couldn't find it.

"*No importa,*" she said. "The beans will taste just as good if I use another spoon."

She added water all day long until the beans were plump and soft. Then she scrubbed the stove and checked the mousetrap.

But it was nowhere in sight!

"*¡Cielos!*" she said. "Heavens! Where is my mind?"

She hurried to the cupboard to fetch another and when it was set and ready to **snap,** she turned off the light and went to bed.

Friday, Rosa María picked up the cake and seven candles.

Tomorrow was the big day. Rosa María knew she mustn't forget anything, so she carefully went over the list one last time.

After dinner she wrapped the cake and checked the mousetrap.

She couldn't believe her eyes.

No mousetrap!

"Thank goodness I've got plenty."

She hurried to the cupboard to fetch another and when it was set and ready to **snap,** she turned off the light and went to bed.

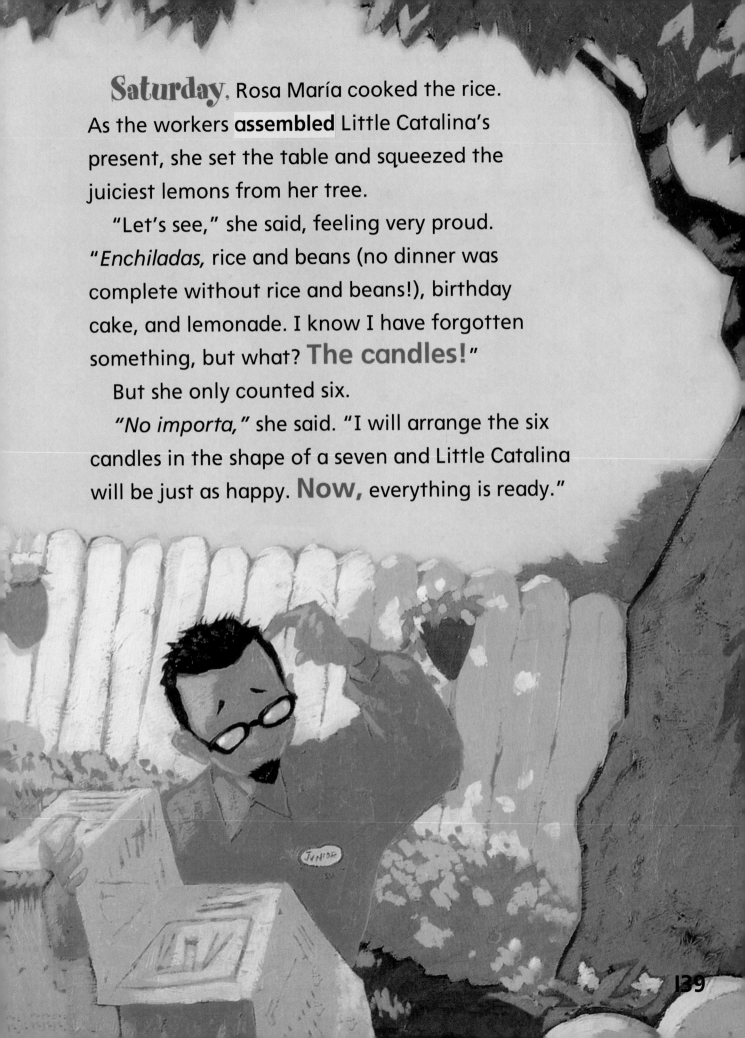

Saturday, Rosa María cooked the rice. As the workers **assembled** Little Catalina's present, she set the table and squeezed the juiciest lemons from her tree.

"Let's see," she said, feeling very proud. "*Enchiladas,* rice and beans (no dinner was complete without rice and beans!), birthday cake, and lemonade. I know I have forgotten something, but what? **The candles!**"

But she only counted six.

"*No importa,*" she said. "I will arrange the six candles in the shape of a seven and Little Catalina will be just as happy. **Now,** everything is ready."

140

But WAS everything ready?

 Fantasy and Reality
Is this story a fantasy or a realistic story? Use details to explain.

That afternoon Rosa María's family filled her tiny *casita.* They ate the *enchiladas* and rice and beans. They drank the fresh-squeezed lemonade. And they **devoured** the cake.

Little Catalina loved her present—a swing set! And after every cousin had a turn, they chanted, "*¡La piñata! ¡La piñata!*"

They ran to the walnut tree and threw a rope over a high branch.

Whack! Whack! Little Catalina swung the *piñata* stick.

"Wait!" cried Rosa María as she remembered what she'd forgotten. But it was too late.

Crack! The *piñata* separated, and the children scrambled to collect the candy.

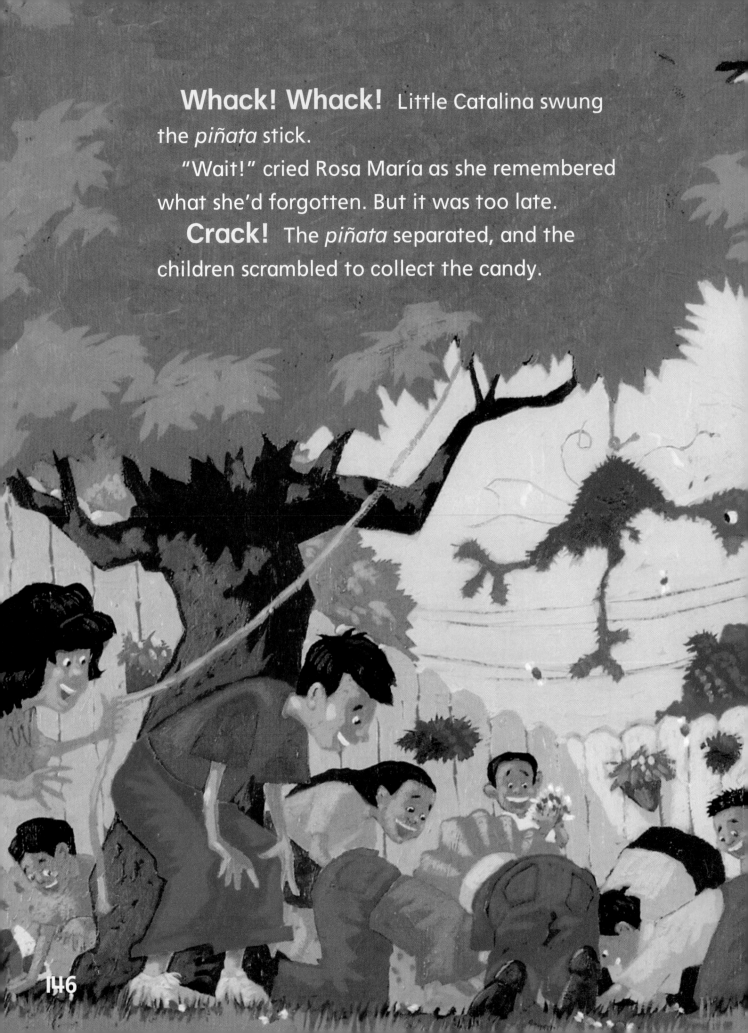

How could that be? Rosa María puzzled.
I must have filled it without even realizing!
She laughed at her own forgetfulness
as she hugged her granddaughter and
said, *"Feliz cumpleaños,* my Little Catalina.
Happy birthday."

After everyone had gone, Rosa María tidied her kitchen and thought contentedly about the *fiesta*. She pictured the happy look on Little Catalina's face when the candy spilled from the *piñata*. But Rosa María still couldn't remember when she had filled it.

"*No importa*," she said. "It was a wonderful day."

But as Rosa María swept out the cupboard, she discovered the telltale signs of mice!

"*¡Ratones!*" she cried. "Where are my mousetraps? I will set them all!"

She inched to the floor and when she did, something caught her eye.

She looked closer.

Maybe I **didn't** fill the *piñata*, she thought.

"Was it possible?" she asked, shaking her head. "Could I have had help?"

Rosa María looked at the leftovers. Too much for one person.

And what was it her mother had always said? "When there's room in the heart, there's room in the house . . . **even** for a mouse."

"*¡Fíjate!* Imagine that!" she said. "I remembered the words wrong all these years."

Besides, how many could there be? Two? Four?

"*No importa,*" she said. "It doesn't matter if a few helpful mice live here, too."

Then she turned off the light and went to bed . . .

. . . and never set another mousetrap again.

Celebrating with Joe Cepeda

Joe Cepeda says that many parties from his childhood looked just like the one in this book. For his son's parties, Joe always finds a special piñata. He has even made a hand-painted piñata stick. He hopes it will become a part of their family traditions.

Joe has received many awards for *Mice and Beans*. He has illustrated more than 15 other children's books. He also does artwork for magazines, newspapers, and businesses.

Other books illustrated by Joe Cepeda

LOG ON ▶ FIND OUT

Illustrator Joe Cepeda
www.macmillanmh.com

Author's Purpose

Joe Cepeda shares what he knows about parties. What traditions do you share in your family? What are some things your family does together? Write a paragraph about one of them.

TEKS Comprehension Check

Retell the Story
Use the Retelling Cards
to retell the story.

Retelling Cards

Think and Compare

1. On what day did Rosa María go to the market? **Facts**

2. Use details from the story to describe which parts of this story could really happen and which could only happen in a fantasy. **Fantasy and Reality**

Reality	Fantasy
What Could Happen?	What Could Not Happen?

3. Why does Rosa María need to **fetch** mousetrap after mousetrap? **Make Inferences**

4. What does the author want readers to know about the mice that live with Rosa María? **Author's Purpose**

5. Pam Muñoz Ryan also wrote *Stirring Up Memories*. How are the setting and plot in *Mice and Beans* similar to that text? How are they different? **Reading/Writing Across Texts**

155

Genre
Some **expository** articles give you information about how to make a food or a drink.

 Text Feature
Written Directions are steps that tell you how to make or do something.

Content Vocabulary
liquids

solids

gas

ROSA MARÍA'S RICE AND BEANS

When you cook, you often mix **liquids** and **solids**, such as when you mix water and flour. These different states of matter can change in different ways as you cook them.

Heating some solids can make them turn brown. Other solids become soft when you heat them. Heating liquids can make them boil. If you boil liquid long enough, it can change its state. It becomes a **gas**, another state of matter.

In the following recipes you will mix solids and liquids to make Rosa María's rice and beans.

Rice

What You Need

2   tablespoons vegetable oil

⅓   cup minced onion

⅓   cup minced bell pepper

1 ½ cups long grain white rice

1   14 ½ -ounce can chicken or vegetable broth

¼   cup tomato sauce stirred into 1 ½ cups of water

What To Do

1. Pour the oil into a large skillet. Oil is a liquid.

2. Add the onion, bell pepper, and rice. These are solids. Sauté (SAW-tay), or fry, these solids over medium heat until rice is lightly toasted, and the vegetables are soft.

3. Add the liquids (broth and tomato sauce water) to the solids. Bring to a boil.

4. Cover, and turn the heat to low.

5. Simmer for 20 to 25 minutes, or until the liquid has been soaked up. Do not stir while simmering or the rice will be mushy.

Beans

What You Need

1	16-ounce bag dried pinto beans
1	large onion, chopped
4	cloves garlic, minced
2	14 ½-ounce cans chicken or vegetable broth
2	14 ½-ounce soup cans of water
	salt and pepper, add to taste

What To Do

1. Follow the directions on the back of the bag for cleaning and soaking the beans.
2. Drain the water (a liquid).
3. Combine the solids (beans, onions, and garlic) with the liquids (broth and water) in a large pot. Bring to a boil.
4. Cover pot. Reduce heat to low and simmer for 2 ½ to 3 hours. Stir often until beans are plump and soft.

Solid, Liquid, or Gas?

The same material can be in three different states—solid, liquid, and gas.

1. A solid has a definite size and shape. Ice is a solid. When water freezes, it becomes ice.

2. Liquid takes up space, but it does not have shape. Liquid in a container takes that container's shape. Water is a liquid.

3. Gas does not take up space or have shape. Steam is a gas. When water boils, it turns to steam.

 Connect and Compare

1. What should you do to the beans while they are simmering? **Written Directions**

2. Think about the recipes and the story *Mice and Beans*. Rosa María planned a menu for the party. Write a menu that includes the food you would like to have at a party.
Reading/Writing Across Texts

 Science Activity

Think of your favorite recipe. Tell a partner the steps of the recipe. Give your instructions in the correct sequence. Describe the solids, liquids, and gases you would see when you made your recipe.

Writing

TEKS Vary Words

Good writers **vary words** to make their writing clear, interesting, and more exact.

I use the word <u>annual</u> to tell how often field day happens.

I vary the words I use to describe the event.

Community Field Day!

The annual Washington Elementary School Field Day will take place on June 18.

Please join us for a day filled with exciting activities and terrific food. The fun starts at 1 p.m. at the school's football field.

This event is open to all students and their families. Take part in sack races, a water balloon toss, and an obstacle course! A picnic will follow the games. Don't miss this event!

Contact Ms. Cahill for more information.

Your Writing Prompt

A flyer or a poster can advertise or tell about an event.

Think about an event in your school or community.

Write an advertisement about this event. Include the need for volunteers.

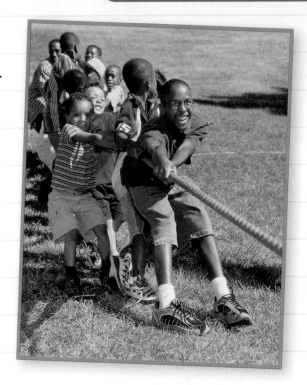

Writer's Checklist

✔ My writing clearly advertises an event.

✔ I give information about what will happen at the event and where it will take place.

☑ I **vary words** to make my writing interesting and clear to readers.

✔ I form contractions correctly. I capitalize and punctuate my sentences in the right places.

TEKS

Review

Cause and Effect
Sequence of Events
Fantasy and Reality
Character
Setting
Synonyms

Chicken Little

One morning Chicken Little walked through the woods. **PLUNK!** An acorn fell on her head.

Chicken Little clucked, "The sky is falling! I must tell the queen!" She took the acorn with her to prove that the sky was falling.

She had not gone far when—**BUMP!**—she ran into Henny Penny.

Chicken Little clucked, "The sky is falling! We must tell the queen."

Chicken Little and Henny Penny ran. They had not gone far when—**THUMP!**—they bumped into Ducky Lucky.

Chicken Little and Henny Penny clucked, "The sky is falling! We must tell the queen."

Chicken Little, Henny Penny, and Ducky Lucky ran. They had not gone far when—**SCREECH!**—the three friends stopped. Standing before them was Foxy Loxy.

Sly Foxy Loxy smiled, showing his sharp teeth. "Good morning," he said. "What is your hurry?"

Chicken Little clucked, "The sky is falling. We must tell the queen."

Foxy Loxy's smile grew. "I will lead you to the queen," he said.

Chicken Little, Henny Penny, and Ducky Lucky followed Foxy Loxy. That crafty fox led them straight to his den. Before he could eat them, he heard the sounds of the queen coming near. Foxy Loxy was very afraid of the queen. He ran far, far away.

Chicken Little, Henny Penny, and Ducky Lucky told the queen about the sky falling. Chicken Little showed her the acorn.

"Silly animals," said the queen. "The sky is not falling. That acorn simply fell from a tree. Go home and do not worry about the sky anymore."

The three friends marched home and did exactly as the queen said.

Foolish, Timid Rabbit

Foolish, timid Rabbit sat under a coconut tree. He looked around the forest and said, "What will happen to me if the world falls apart?"

KERPLUNK! A coconut crashed behind Rabbit.

Rabbit cried, "The world is falling apart!" He hopped away, yelling loudly.

Soon another rabbit saw him. "What are you yelling about?"

Rabbit cried, "The world is falling apart!" He hopped away, screaming even louder.

Soon the word spread from one rabbit to the next. In no time at all other forest animals heard the scary news. Deer told Buffalo. Buffalo told Rhinoceros. Rhinoceros told Elephant. Now all the animals were running and screaming.

Suddenly Lion stepped quietly from his cave. "Stop a moment, friends. Why are you running so fast?"

"The world is falling apart!" cried Rabbit. "I heard the first piece fall."

Lion nodded wisely. "Show me where it fell," he said.

Rabbit led Lion to the coconut tree.

Lion laughed when he saw the coconut on the ground. "Rabbit," he said. "You only heard a coconut fall. The world is safe and all in one piece. Do not bother the other animals with your nonsense."

"Foolish Rabbit," scolded the other animals. "If not for wise Lion, we would be running away forever."

Comprehension

Monitor and Adjust Comprehension

- Good readers monitor and adjust comprehension to better understand text in an article or story. You can monitor comprehension by rereading, using background knowledge, and creating images in your mind.

- With a partner, reread parts of *Head, Body, Legs* on pages 10–35. Discuss with your partner how rereading helps you understand the lesson learned in this folktale.

Writing

Write a Friendly Letter

- Write a letter to a friend or family member about a class project you have worked on. Share details about your story. Be sure to put your ideas in the correct sequence. Include a date, greeting, and closing.

Word Study

Phonics

Vowel Digraphs and Diphthongs

- Say each of the following words aloud: *glue, suit, flew, soil, growling, ground, royal,* and *toy.* Review the sound each word makes. Then on a separate piece of paper, list each word. Next to each word write a word that rhymes with it.

Spelling

Words with Vowel Digraphs and Diphthongs

- Review words: *draw, mushroom, crawling, growl, sidewalk, hook, jaw, gnaw, sauce, jigsaw, around, moist,* and *enjoy.* Write each word on a piece of paper.

- On a separate piece of paper, write questions for each word. Then exchange papers with a partner. Ask your partner to answer each question. Have them write and underline the word in their answer.

The
Big
Question

How do animals
and plants change
as they grow?

LOG ON ▶ VIEW IT

Theme Video
Growing and Changing
www.macmillanmh.com

169

How do animals and plants change as they grow?

Animals and plants go through specific changes during their lives. Some baby animals, such as kittens or bear cubs, look a lot like their parents. Other animals change a lot as they grow up, as a caterpillar changes into a butterfly. Plants change as they grow, too. Many plants start out as seeds. The seeds send roots into the ground and stems up through the earth and into the air. These stems develop leaves and flowers, which contain seeds for new plants. Learning about animals and plants will help you care for them and better understand the natural world around you.

Research Activities

During this unit you will help gather information. As a class we will make a list of topics and create open-ended questions. Research one plant or animal. Then create a Life Cycle Booklet for your choice.

Keep Track of Ideas

As you read, keep track of all you are learning about how animals and plants change and grow. Use the **Two-Pocket Foldable**. On the left pocket, write "Plants." On the right pocket, write "Animals." Each week record plant and animal facts on cards and put them in the appropriate pocket.

Growing and Changing

Plants   Animals

FOLDABLES®
Study Organizer

Digital Learning

LOG ON ▶ **FIND OUT** www.macmillanmh.com

StudentWorks Plus™
Interactive Student Book

- **Research Roadmap**
  Follow a step-by-step guide to complete your research project.

Texas Online Resources

- Topic Finder and Other Research Tools
- Videos and Virtual Field Trips
- Photos and Drawings for Presentations
- Related Articles and Web Resources
- Texas Web Site Links

All About TEXAS

Ned Fritz

Edward "Ned" Fritz was an environmentalist who helped form many groups in Texas that save forests and endangered species.

Talk About It

How do plants change as they grow?

LOG ON ▶ VIEW IT

Oral Language Activities
Plant Life
www.macmillanmh.com

A Plant's Life

Vocabulary

burst

drifts

desert

drowns

gently

neighbor

TEKS Context Clues

To clarify information in a text, use context clues in sentences to help you figure out the meaning of an unfamiliar word.

Jen is my *neighbor*. She lives next door.

Plant Power!

by Bradley Roberts

People use plants in many ways. All around us are objects that come from plants.

Your T-shirt probably started as a cotton plant. The cotton plant has seeds called bolls. Hot weather makes the bolls **burst**. When they break open, a soft fluff of cotton pops out. The fluff sometimes **drifts** in the air, moving slowly in the wind. People can spin the fluff into thread that becomes material.

Other plants are used to make medicines. Some of these plants are found in a dry, hot place like the **desert**. The aloe plant has a juice that helps heal cuts. Many people grow aloe plants. An aloe plant **drowns** easily. It is important not to give the plant too much water because it will die. To get the aloe juice, **gently** break off a leaf. Do it carefully so as not to harm the plant.

Some plants are so big that we can build with them. Many houses are made from trees. Look at the houses of the people who live near you. Does your **neighbor** have a wooden house?

Reread for **Comprehension**

Summarize

Draw Conclusions

After you summarize this article, you can use the most important facts or ideas to help draw conclusions. Reread the article and use the chart to draw conclusions about why plants are important to humans.

Fact	Fact

↓

Conclusion

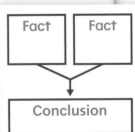

LOG ON ▶ LEARN IT Comprehension
www.macmillanmh.com

Comprehension

Genre
Informational Fiction is a made-up story that may give information about a real-life topic.

Summarize

Draw Conclusions As you read, use your Conclusions Chart.

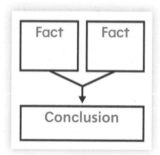

Read to Find Out Set your own purpose. What do you want to find out about the tiny seed?

Award Winning Author

The Tiny Seed

It is Autumn.
A strong wind is blowing. It blows flower seeds
high in the air and carries them far across
the land. One of the seeds is tiny,
smaller than any of the others.
Will it be able to keep up with the others?
And where are they all going?

One of the seeds flies higher than the others.
Up, up it goes! It flies too high and the sun's rays
burn it up. But the tiny seed sails on with the others.

TEKS Draw Conclusions
How does the wind help
the seed?

Another seed lands on a tall and icy mountain.
The ice never melts, and the seed cannot grow.
The rest of the seeds fly on. But the tiny seed
does not go as fast as the others.

Now they fly over the ocean.
One seed falls into the water and **drowns**.
The others sail on with the wind.
But the tiny seed does not go as high as
the others.

One seed **drifts** down onto the **desert**.
It is hot and dry, and the seed cannot grow.
Now the tiny seed is flying very low,
but the wind pushes it on with the others.

Finally the wind stops and the seeds fall **gently**
down on the ground. A bird comes by
and eats one seed. The tiny seed is not eaten.
It is so small that the bird does not see it.

Now it is Winter.

After their long trip the seeds settle down.
They look just as if they are going to sleep
in the earth. Snow falls and covers them
like a soft white blanket. A hungry mouse
that also lives in the ground eats a seed
for his lunch. But the tiny seed lies very still
and the mouse does not see it.

Now it is Spring.

After a few months the snow has melted.
It is really Spring! Birds fly by. The sun shines.
Rain falls. The seeds grow so round and full
they start to **burst** open a little. Now they
are not seeds any more. They are plants.
First they send roots down into the earth.
Then their little stems and leaves begin to grow
up toward the sun and air. There is another plant
that grows much faster than the new little
plants. It is a big fat weed. And it takes all
the sunlight and the rain away from one of
the small new plants. And that little plant dies.

 Locate Facts
Locating facts is a useful strategy
to help understand the story. What
do the seeds become after they
burst open?

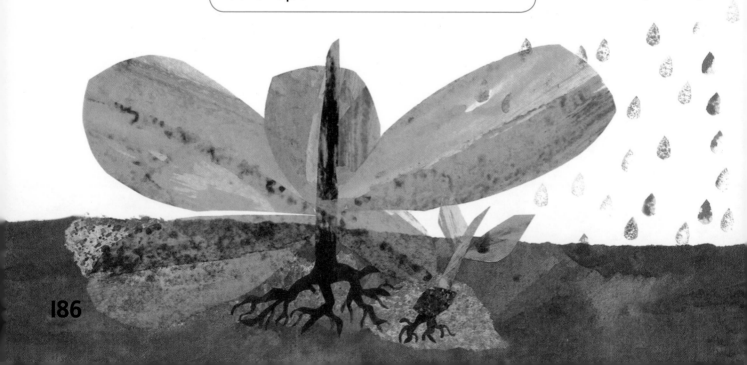

The tiny seed hasn't begun to grow yet.
It will be too late! Hurry!
But finally it too starts to grow into a plant.

The warm weather also brings the children
out to play. They too have been waiting
for the sun and spring time. One child doesn't
see the plants as he runs along and—Oh!
He breaks one! Now it cannot grow any more.

The tiny plant that grew from the tiny seed is growing fast, but its **neighbor** grows even faster. Before the tiny plant has three leaves the other plant has seven! And look! A bud! And now even a flower!

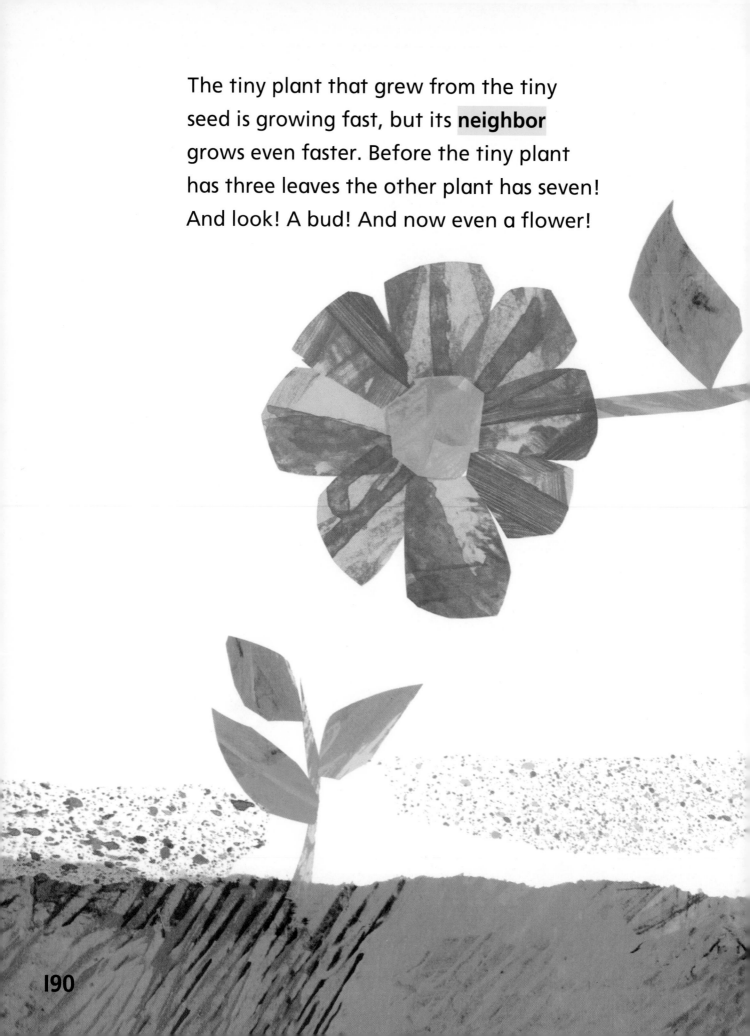

But what is happening? First there are footsteps.
Then a shadow looms over them. Then a hand
reaches down and breaks off the flower.
A boy has picked the flower to give to a friend.

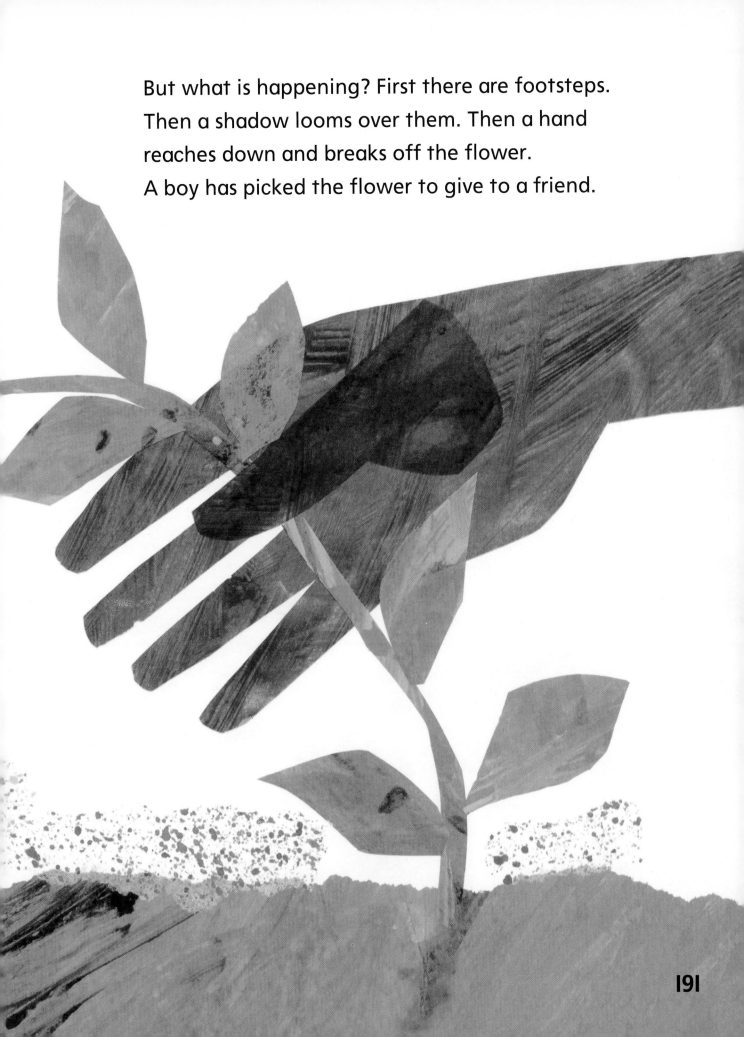

It is Summer.

Now the tiny plant from the tiny seed
is all alone. It grows on and on. It doesn't stop.
The sun shines on it and the rain waters it.
It has many leaves. It grows taller and taller.
It is taller than the people. It is taller than
the trees. It is taller than the houses.
And now a flower grows on it. People come
from far and near to look at this flower.
It is the tallest flower they have ever seen.
It is a giant flower.

All summer long the birds and bees and butterflies come visiting. They have never seen such a big and beautiful flower.

Now it is Autumn again.

The days grow shorter. The nights grow cooler. And the wind carries yellow and red leaves past the flower. Some petals drop from the giant flower and they sail along with the bright leaves over the land and down to the ground.

TEKS Draw Conclusions
Use details from the text to help draw a conclusion about what may happen to the flower next.

197

The wind blows harder. The flower has lost almost all of its petals. It sways and bends away from the wind. But the wind grows stronger and shakes the flower. Once more the wind shakes the flower, and this time the flower's seed pod opens. Out come many tiny seeds that quickly sail far away on the wind.

Cut, Paste, and Learn with Eric Carle

Eric Carle has illustrated more than 70 books. He wrote most of these books, too. Many books, such as *The Tiny Seed*, are about nature.

Eric's artwork is called *collage*. First he paints on paper. Then he cuts it into small shapes. He glues the painted paper in layers to make the larger shapes he wants.

Eric says, "I want to show [children] that learning is really both fascinating and fun."

Other books written and illustrated by Eric Carle

Author Eric Carle
www.macmillanmh.com

Author's Purpose
Eric Carle explains what happens to a seed. Think about a flower, plant, or tree. Describe what the plant looks like and how it grows.

☑TEKS Comprehension Check

Retell the Story

Use the Retelling Cards to retell the story.

Retelling Cards

Think and Compare

1. When do the tiny seeds burst open? **Details**

2. How does being very small help the tiny seed? **Draw Conclusions**

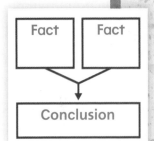

Fact	Fact

Conclusion

3. What will happen to the tiny seed each season? **Make Inferences**

4. What does the author want readers to learn about nature? **Author's Purpose**

5. "Plant Power!" on pages 174–175 tells about how cotton bolls **burst**. Based on what you learned in *The Tiny Seed*, how do cotton seeds get spread around? **Reading/Writing Across Texts**

Plant Parts

by Pilar Jacob

A plant is a living thing. It uses its many parts to grow from a small **seed** to a large plant. Each part helps the plant stay healthy. Plants also need **sunlight** to grow. They get light from the sun and **minerals** from the soil. These things help the plant to stay alive and grow.

Flowers
Flowers make seeds that can grow into new plants.

Stem
The stem helps hold up the plant. It moves the food and water from the roots to the other parts of the plant.

Leaves
Leaves use sunlight, water, and air to make food.

Roots
A plant grows roots under the ground. The roots hold the plant in place.

Fruit

Some plants have fruit. The fruit grows around the seeds and keeps them safe.

Seeds

Seeds can grow into new plants.

 Connect and Compare

1. Choose two parts of a plant. Tell a partner how each part helps the plant. **Diagrams and Labels**

2. Look at the picture of the giant flower at the end of *The Tiny Seed*. Draw a picture that looks like this flower. Label each part of the plant. **Reading/Writing Across Texts**

Science Activity

Research a plant that grows fruit. Use the information to make a diagram of this plant and label each part.

 LOG ON ▶ **FIND OUT** Science Plants
www.macmillanmh.com

Reading and Writing Connection

Writing

TEKS Important Details

Details can give readers **important** information on how to do something.

These details tell what I will need to do this project.

These steps give details about how best to grow the flowers.

How to Grow Marigolds

You will need marigold seeds, a pot with soil, and water.

marigold seeds   pot with soil   water

1. Make two holes in the soil about two inches apart. Make each hole one inch deep.

2. Put two seeds in each hole. Cover them with soil.

3. Put the pot in a sunny place.

4. Water it about every four days. Watch your marigolds grow!

Your Writing Prompt

A poster can show how to do something.

Think about what you know how to do and would like to share.

Make a poster. Write the steps that tell what to do. Draw pictures with labels to show what is needed.

Writer's Checklist

✓ My writing is about how to do something.

✓ I include numbered steps that show the correct order of how to do something.

✓ I include **important details** that help the reader know exactly what to do.

✓ My sentences are complete. I use the correct end punctuation. I use pronouns correctly.

Garden Plants

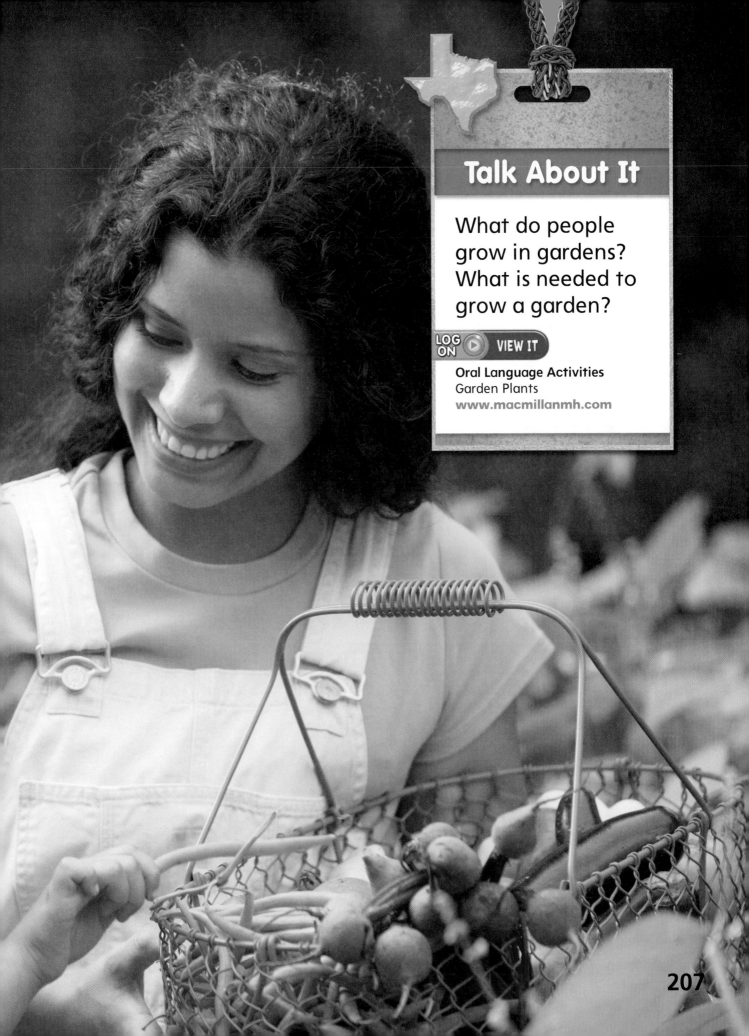

Talk About It

What do people grow in gardens? What is needed to grow a garden?

LOG ON ▶ **VIEW IT**

Oral Language Activities
Garden Plants
www.macmillanmh.com

207

scent

trade

muscles

prickly

blooming

aroma

 Content Clues

Homophones are words that sound the same but have different spellings and different meanings.

Scent and *cent* are homophones.

Scent means "smell." A *cent* is money.

City Garden

by Roberto Salazar

When we lived in the country, Dad and I had a garden. We planted beans, peas, and other vegetables. To us the **scent** of moist soil and growing plants was a kind of perfume. We loved the earthy smell.

Then we moved to the city. We had to **trade** our big country garden for a small city window box.

Dad and I missed the garden. So he offered to help my class plant a garden in an empty lot.

First, my class dug up the soil in the lot. We needed strong **muscles** to do all that hard work.

Next, we planted seeds and small plants in neat rows. We wore gloves because some plants had sharp, **prickly** thorns.

Soon the flowers were **blooming**. The lot reminded me of my old garden. It was great to smell the fresh **aroma** of plants that filled the air. Then tiny vegetables grew. Last, the vegetables became large and ripe, so we picked them. Dad and I enjoyed some tasty vegetables from our city garden.

Reread for **Comprehension**

Summarize

Sequence of Events When you sequence events in a story, you put the events in the order that they took place. Identify what happened first, next, and last. Putting events in sequence can help you summarize a story. Reread the selection and use the Sequence Chart to describe the sequence of events.

First
↓
Next
↓
Last

LOG ON ▶ LEARN IT Comprehension
www.macmillanmh.com

Comprehension

Genre
Fiction is a story with made-up characters and events.

Summarize
Sequence of Events
As you read the story, use the Sequence Chart.

First

↓

Next

↓

Last

Read to Find Out
How does the garden change from the beginning to the end of the story?

The Ugly Vegetables

by Grace Lin

Award Winning Selection

In the spring I helped my mother start our garden.
We used tall shovels to turn the grass upside down,
and I saw pink worms wriggle around. It was hard work.
When we stopped to rest, we saw that the neighbors
were starting their gardens too.

"Hello, Irma!" my mother called to Mrs. Crumerine.
Mrs. Crumerine was digging too. She was using a small
shovel, one that fit in her hand.

"Mommy," I asked, "why are we using such big
shovels? Mrs. Crumerine has a small one."

"Because our garden needs more digging," she said.

I helped my mother plant the seeds, and we dragged the hose to the garden. "Hi, Linda! Hi, Mickey!" I called to the Fitzgeralds. They were sprinkling water on their garden with green watering cans.

"Mommy," I asked, "why are we using a hose? Linda and Mickey use watering cans."

"Because our garden needs more water," she said.

213

Then my mother drew funny pictures on pieces of paper, and I stuck them into the garden.

"Hello, Roseanne!" my mother called across the street to Mrs. Angelhowe.

"Mommy," I asked, "why are we sticking these papers in the garden? Mrs. Angelhowe has seed packages in her garden."

"Because our garden is going to grow Chinese vegetables," she told me. "These are the names of the vegetables in Chinese, so I can tell which plants are growing where."

One day I saw our garden growing. Little green stems that looked like grass had popped out from the ground.

"Our garden's growing!" I yelled. "Our garden's growing!"

I rushed over to the neighbors' gardens to see if theirs had grown. Their plants looked like little leaves.

"Mommy," I asked, "why do our plants look like grass? The neighbors' plants look different."

"Because they are growing flowers," she said.

"Why can't we grow flowers?" I asked.

"These are better than flowers," she said.

Soon all the neighbors' gardens were **blooming**.

Up and down the street grew rainbows of flowers.

The wind always smelled sweet, and butterflies and bees flew everywhere. Everyone's garden was beautiful, except for ours.

Ours was all dark green and ugly.

"Why didn't we grow flowers?" I asked again.

"These are better than flowers," Mommy said again.

I looked, but saw only black-purple-green vines, fuzzy wrinkled leaves, **prickly** stems, and a few little yellow flowers.

"I don't think so," I said.

"You wait and see," Mommy said.

Before long, our vegetables grew. Some were big
and lumpy. Some were thin and green and covered
with bumps. Some were just plain icky yellow. They
were ugly vegetables.

TEKS Sequence of Events
Use details from the story
to describe the sequence of
events so far.

219

Sometimes I would go over to the neighbors' and look
at their pretty gardens. They would show the poppies and
peonies and petunias to me, and I would feel sad that our
garden wasn't as nice.

One day my mother and I picked the vegetables from
the garden. We filled a whole wheelbarrow full of them.
We wheeled them to the kitchen. My mother washed
them and took a big knife and started to chop them.

"Aie-yow!" she said when she cut them. She had to use all her **muscles**. The vegetables were hard and tough.

"This is a sheau hwang gua," Mommy said, handing me a bumpy, curled vegetable. She pointed at the other vegetables. "This is shiann tsay. That's a torng hau."

 TEKS **Sequence of Events**
Describe how the girl's mother prepares the vegetables. Put the steps in the correct sequence.

I went outside to play. While I was playing catch with Mickey, a magical **aroma** filled the air. I saw the neighbors standing on their porches with their eyes closed, smelling the sky. They took deep breaths of air, like they were trying to eat the smell.

 TEKS **Locate Facts**
One useful strategy is to locate facts. Look at page 222. What are the names of the Chinese vegetables that the girl and her mother picked?

The wind carried it up and down the street.
Even the bees and the butterflies seemed to smell
the **scent** in the breeze.

I smelled it too. It made me hungry, and it was coming from my house!

When I followed it to my house, my mother was putting a big bowl of soup on the table. The soup was yellow and red and green and pink.

"This is a special soup," Mommy said, and she smiled.

She gave me a small bowl full of it and I tasted it. It was so good! The flavors of the soup seemed to dance in my mouth and laugh all the way down to my stomach. I smiled.

"Do you like it?" Mommy asked me.

I nodded and held out my bowl for some more.

"It's made from our vegetables," she told me.

Then the doorbell rang, and we ran to open the door.

All our neighbors were standing at the door
holding flowers.

"We noticed you were cooking." Mr. Fitzgerald
laughed as he held out his flowers. "And we thought
maybe you might be interested in a **trade**!"

We laughed too, and my mother gave them each
their own bowl of her special soup.

My mother told them what each vegetable was
and how she grew it. She gave them the soup recipe
and put some soup into jars for them to take home.
I ate five bowls of soup.

It was the best dinner ever.

The next spring, when my mother was
starting her garden, we planted some flowers
next to the Chinese vegetables. Mrs. Crumerine,
the Fitzgeralds, and the Angelhowes planted
some Chinese vegetables next to their flowers.

Soon the whole neighborhood was growing
Chinese vegetables in their gardens. Up and
down the street, little green plants poked out of
the ground. Some looked like leaves and some
looked like grass, and when the flowers started
blooming, you could smell soup in the air.

In the Garden with Grace Lin

As a girl, **Grace Lin** wanted to be an ice skater. She drew many pictures of herself skating. But when Grace tried to skate, she often fell on her face. Then she looked at the pictures she had drawn. "Maybe I'll be an artist," Grace thought.

Grace says that *The Ugly Vegetables* is based on her childhood. "My mother used to grow Chinese vegetables in her garden while all the neighbors grew flowers. Year after year, I looked with disgust at our ugly garden and asked, 'Why can't we grow flowers?' My mother always answered, 'Because these are better than flowers.' I never agreed, until one day…."

Other books written and illustrated by Grace Lin

Author Grace Lin
www.macmillanmh.com

Author's Purpose

Grace Lin tells a story about how she changed her mind about something. Write about a time you changed your mind about something important to you.

Comprehension Check

Retell the Story

Use the Retelling Cards to retell the story.

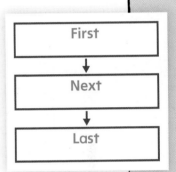

Retelling Cards

Think and Compare

1. When do the girl and her mother begin planting their garden? **Facts**

First
↓
Next
↓
Last

2. Use details from the story to describe the steps the girl and her mother take to grow their garden. **Sequence of Events**

3. How does the girl feel about her vegetable garden? **Make Inferences**

4. At the end of the story, the neighbors plant Chinese vegetables next to their flowers. What does the author want readers to learn? **Author's Purpose**

5. Explain why the boy in "City Garden," on pages 208–209, might like the garden in *The Ugly Vegetables*. **Reading/Writing Across Texts**

233

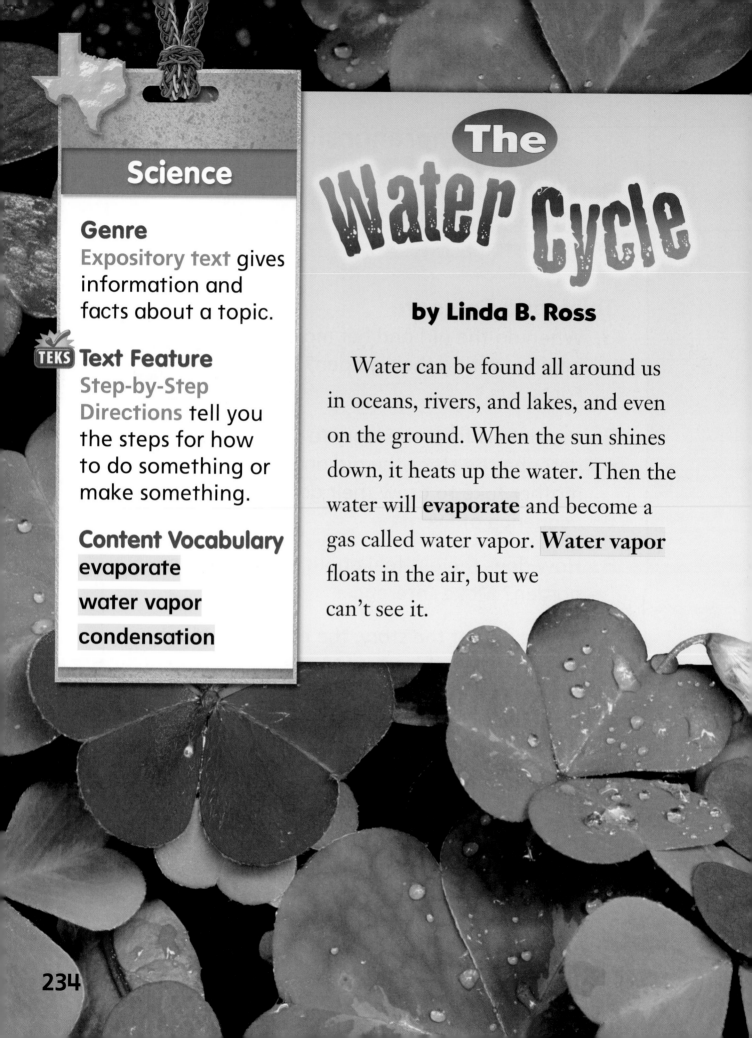

The Water Cycle

by Linda B. Ross

Water can be found all around us in oceans, rivers, and lakes, and even on the ground. When the sun shines down, it heats up the water. Then the water will **evaporate** and become a gas called water vapor. **Water vapor** floats in the air, but we can't see it.

When water vapor rises in the air, it cools off and changes into tiny drops of water. This is called **condensation**. As the tiny drops get bigger and come together, they form clouds.

When the water drops get too heavy, they come down as rain. If the air happens to be very cold, then snow, sleet, or hail may fall.

Rain, snow, sleet, and hail are all forms of water. This water wets the earth and fills our oceans, rivers, and lakes once again. That is how the water cycle keeps going. It is a journey that never ends.

How the Water Cycle Works

Condensation occurs when water vapor forms clouds.

Water falls as rain, snow, sleet, or hail.

Water evaporates.

Oceans / Lakes / Rivers / Groundwater

Evaporation Experiment:
Disappearing Drops

Follow the step-by-step directions to do this experiment. You will see how water changes its form and evaporates.

1. On a sheet of waxed paper, sprinkle a few drops of water.

2. Put the waxed paper in the freezer for about 15 minutes.

3. Take the waxed paper out of the freezer. The drops of water should now be ice.

4. Put the waxed paper outside in a sunny spot.

5. Watch the frozen drops change into water drops again.

6. Continue to watch as the water drops disappear by evaporating into the air.

◀ An ice cube is water in a different form.

Water is an important part of our environment. All living things—plants, animals, and people—need water to live.

The water cycle helps water move through our environment.

 Connect and Compare

1. What happens in step 5 of the experiment? What do the water drops become? **Step-by-Step Directions**

2. Think about this selection and *The Ugly Vegetables*. What smell floated through the air? Explain how this happened. **Reading/Writing Across Texts**

Science Activity

As a class, we will make a list of ways we can conserve water. Choose one example and illustrate a poster showing how people can save water.

LOG ON ▶ FIND OUT **Science** Water Cycle
www.macmillanmh.com

TEKS Sequence of Events

Good writers use **sequence of events** to show the correct order of events in a story.

Reading and Writing Connection

I tell about the first event at the beginning of my story.

The Garden Project
by Lydia P.

Mom and I were working in the garden when I remembered my *science* project. "Oh no! I need an idea for my *science* project," I told her. "It's due next week."

"Why don't you think about it while you water the garden?" Mom said.

As I watered the garden, I looked at the different plants in each row. I noticed that the plants had grown since we planted them last month.

The end tells about the last event in the story.

I ran over to my mother and said, "My project idea is all set. I will show different *seeds* and what the plants look like after they have grown up!"

238

Your Writing Prompt

A garden can be an interesting setting for a story.

Think about a real or make-believe garden.

Now write a story that takes place in this garden.

Writer's Checklist

☑ My writing clearly presents a story about a garden.

☑ The **sequence of events** in my story is clear, with a logical beginning, middle, and end.

☑ I use descriptive details to make my story more interesting.

☑ My sentences are complete and end with the correct punctuation mark. I use pronouns correctly.

How do we learn about animals that lived long, long ago?

LOG ON ▶ **VIEW IT**

Oral Language Activities
Animals Long Ago
www.macmillanmh.com

ANIMALS LONG AGO

Coelacanth

Vocabulary

ancient
hopeful
unable
site
confirm
valid

AFRICA

Madagascar

● Coelacanth
Fish Location

A VERY OLD FISH

The coelacanth (SEE-luh-kanth) is an ancient fish. It lived about 360 million years ago. People first learned about the coelacanth by studying its fossils. Fossils are the shapes or remains left behind by something that lived a long time ago.

People believed that the coelacanths died millions of years ago. But in 1938, a fisherman caught a coelacanth near Madagascar. Since then more have been caught. Now scientists are hopeful they can protect coelacanths. They believe they can help because the scientists have learned more about the fish. They know that coelacanths are unable to live in the warm water near the top of the ocean. The fish can only live deep underwater.

Scientists made a model of the lizard that lived millions of years ago.

This fossil is the head of the ancient lizard.

BOY FINDS FOSSILS!

In 1999, twelve-year-old Miguel Avelas amazed scientists all over the world. Miguel discovered hundreds of fossils in Patagonia, in the southern part of South America. Miguel led scientists to the **site** where he found the fossils. The scientists guessed the fossils were from a lizard.

The scientists studied the fossils and were able to **confirm** that their idea was correct. The fossils gave them **valid** information that this lizard had lived more than 120 million years ago. Now they also had proof that this lizard had lived in Patagonia. Miguel's discovery gave the scientists important new information.

Meet the Super Croc

Genre
Expository text gives information about real people, things, or events.

Adjust Reading Rate

TEKS Summarize
To summarize a selection, you tell only the most important ideas without retelling the whole selection.

Did a crocodile the size of a school bus once live on Earth?

What kind of animal was it? Its body was about 40 feet long. That's about the size of a school bus. Its jaws were about 5 feet long. That's about as long as some people are tall! It had about 100 teeth.

Name: *Sarcosuchus imperator* ("Super Croc")
Length: Up to 50 feet
Weight: About 17,500 pounds
Lived: About 110 million years ago

This powerful creature hid in the water, waiting for an animal to come to the river for a drink. Any animal that was grabbed by those teeth would be **unable** to get away.

Don't worry! This toothy giant is no longer alive today. It lived about 110 million years ago, when dinosaurs roamed Earth. That's about 105 million years before human beings were around.

This drawing shows what scientists think "Super Croc" looked like.

Name: **Australian crocodile**
Length: **Up to 23 feet**
Weight: **About 2,000 pounds**
Lived: **Alive today**

Name: **American alligator**
Length: **Up to 20 feet**
Weight: **About 1,300 pounds**
Lived: **Alive today**

245

Paul Sereno, a scientist, was the leader of a team of scientists who found the bones of the animal. They discovered them at a **site** in Niger, a country in Africa.

Sereno and his team were **hopeful** the bones belonged to a kind of giant crocodile from the time of the dinosaurs. But they weren't sure. The whole team needed to study the bones before they could **confirm** their theory. They compared the bones to the bodies of crocodiles living today. If the bones were similar, the theory would be **valid**.

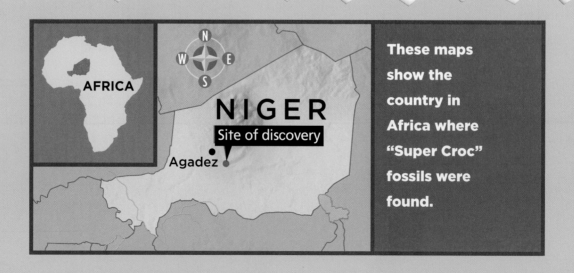

AFRICA

NIGER
Site of discovery

Agadez

These maps show the country in Africa where "Super Croc" fossils were found.

246

The shape of the head and skull bones gave Sereno and his team the proof they were looking for. The **ancient** bones belonged to a "Super Croc" that lived at the same time the dinosaurs lived on Earth.

Sereno made copies of the bones to keep in the United States. The original bones were sent back to the country of Niger. If you want to see the real "Super Croc," the bones are on display in a museum there.

A young boy checks out the model of "Super Croc."

TEKS Think and Compare

1. What type of bones did Paul Sereno find?

2. What steps were taken to prove Sereno's theory?

3. How would you summarize this selection?

4. Compare the creature described in "Boy Finds Fossils!" with "Super Croc." How are they the same? How are they different?

Some Strange Teeth

Answering Questions
Sometimes the answer is on the page. Sometimes it is not. You must look for clues.

Scientist David Krause digs for fossils on Madagascar.

❶ Dinosaur fossil hunters were digging in Madagascar. It is an island off the coast of Africa. The team found something that looked like the lower jaw of an animal. It had strange sharp teeth. Was it a dinosaur bone?

❷ "We thought it could be a crocodile or a flying reptile," the team leader said. Scientists studied the hook-shaped teeth. The team discovered that this animal was a dinosaur that lived 70 million years ago and ate fish and insects. For a dinosaur, it was not very big.

❸ Madagascar is a good place for finding dinosaur bones. The oldest dinosaur bones ever found were dug up there. Scientists will keep looking. One scientist said, "We still don't know everything about dinosaurs."

DIRECTIONS

Decide which is the best answer to each question.

1 Fossil hunters found a —

  A team of scientists

  B crocodile tooth

  C flying reptile

  D small dinosaur jaw

2 Where did they dig?

  A the coast of Africa

  B Madagascar

  C a dinosaur museum

  D 70 million years ago

3 What is the article mainly about?

  A Madagascar, an island in Africa

  B African animals with sharp teeth

  C Dinosaurs that ate fish and insects

  D Scientists who look for dinosaur fossils

4 What is the best summary of the selection?

  A Fossil hunters found a jaw with sharp teeth. It was from a dinosaur that lived 70 million years ago.

  B Scientists live in Madagascar. That is where all the dinosaur bones are found.

  C Fish, crocodiles, and insects have sharp teeth. They are like dinosaurs.

  D Dinosaurs were not very big. They had sharp teeth and strong jaws to eat fish and insects.

Write to a Prompt

Tina wrote about a time when teamwork helped her to find her cat.

My story has a beginning, a middle, and an ending.

Finding Peanut

One day I could not find my cat Peanut. He stays in the house most of the time, but sometimes he goes into the yard.

Peanut was not in the house. He was not in the yard. I looked all over and called his name. Soon my friend Tracy next door heard me. She said, "Can I help?"

"You go that way," I said. "I'll go this way." I did not see Peanut anywhere.

After a while Tracy came around the corner carrying Peanut! "He was in a tree," Tracy said. "A big dog was barking at him."

I thanked Tracy. I might not have found Peanut without her help.

Writing Prompt

Respond in writing to the prompt below. Review the hints below before and after you write.

Write about a time when you worked with a partner or a team.

Writing Hints

- ☑ Remember to write about a time when you worked with a partner or team.

- ☑ Plan your writing by organizing your ideas.

- ☑ Include important details to support your ideas.

- ☑ Check that each sentence you write helps readers to understand your writing.

- ☑ Use correct spelling, capitalization, punctuation, and grammar.

- ☑ Review and edit your writing.

Special
Animals

Talk About It

How do animals change as they grow?

LOG ON ▶ VIEW IT

Oral Language Activities
Special Animals
www.macmillanmh.com

Leo Grows Up

by Kevin Lee

Leo was a playful kitten. He loved to chase and play with his friends. But sometimes the other kittens weren't nice.

"Look at Leo," they said. "Why is he so big?" The kittens **giggled**. Leo heard their laughs. He felt he didn't fit in with the other kittens.

Once a bird **fluttered** by him, flapping its wings as it passed by.

"I wish I was like a bird," said Leo. "I would be light and tiny."

Leo left the kittens. He explored the jungle on his own for many months. Leo grew taller. His fur became thicker.

One day Leo heard a roar behind a bush. He stopped and **peered** over it. When he looked over the top, Leo saw animals that he **recognized**. He knew he had seen them before. They looked just like him, but bigger!

The giant cats ran away. They **vanished** into the trees so Leo couldn't see them anymore. He ran after them. "Look, it's another lion," one of the big cats said.

Then Leo knew why he was bigger than the other kittens. He was a lion, not a cat! That night Leo **snuggled** with the other lions. They slept close together. Finally Leo belonged.

Reread for **Comprehension**

Reread

TEKS **Make Inferences** Authors do not always tell readers all that happens. But they give clues. Readers use these clues to make inferences. When you make inferences, you figure out how a character feels, or what is taking place. Rereading parts of a story can help you seek clarification and find clues to make inferences.

What I Read	What I Know

→ Inference

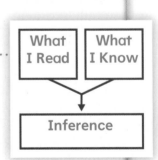

LOG ON ▶ LEARN IT Comprehension
www.macmillanmh.com

Comprehension

Genre
Fantasy is a story that has made-up characters, settings, or other things that could not happen in real life.

Reread
TEKS Make Inferences
As you read, use your Inference Chart.

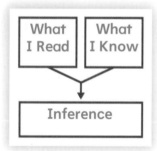

Read to Find Out
How do you know Farfallina and Marcel are good friends?

Farfallina & Marcel

by Holly Keller

Award Winning Author

The rain fell all morning.
It splattered on the pond and
splashed on Farfallina's leaf.
She found a dry spot and ate it.
"Hey," said a little voice.
"You're eating my umbrella."
Farfallina **peered** over the edge.
A small gray bird was huddled underneath.

Farfallina liked his soft feathers and his gentle eyes.

"I'm Farfallina," she said,

and she slid down to the ground.

"My name is Marcel," said the bird.

He liked Farfallina's smile and her pretty colors.

The rain turned to drizzle, and Farfallina wanted to play.

"I'll hide and you find me," she said.

Marcel agreed.

Farfallina hid under a fern close to the ground

because she knew that Marcel couldn't climb.

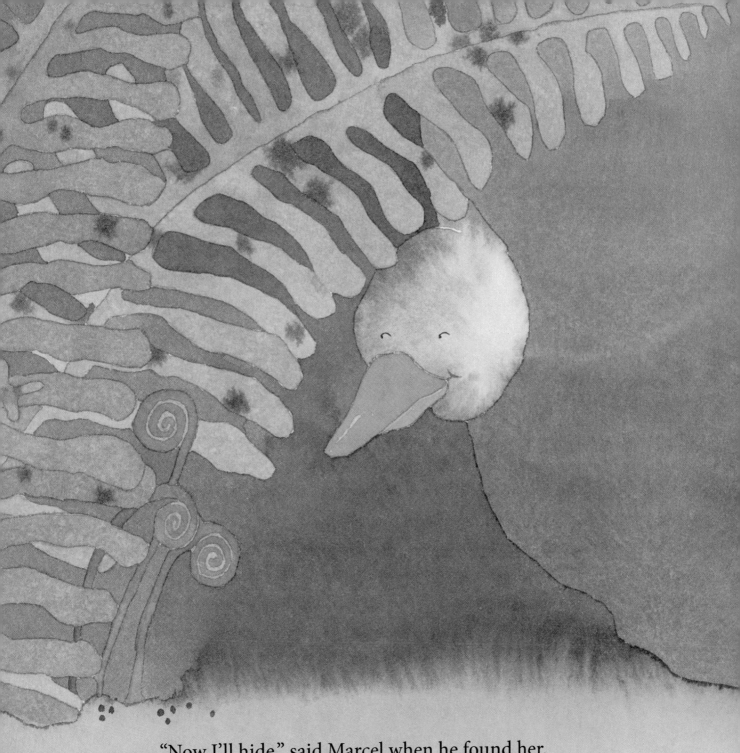

"Now I'll hide," said Marcel when he found her.
And he hid right behind the tree
because he knew that Farfallina moved slowly.

TEKS Make Inferences
Use clues from the story to make an inference about the way Farfallina and Marcel feel about each other.

"I can take you for a ride on the pond," said Marcel.

Farfallina inched her way up to Marcel's back.

"You tickle," said Marcel, and he slipped into the water.

Farfallina **giggled**.

"There's so much to see," she said.

Farfallina and Marcel played together every day.

They liked the same games, and they liked each other.

But one day Farfallina was not herself.

"I'm not sick," she told Marcel, "just a little uncomfortable.
I need to climb up onto a branch and rest for a while."

"I'll wait for you," Marcel called as Farfallina made
her way up the tree.

Marcel watched until Farfallina was completely
out of sight. Then he settled himself in the grass
and waited.

Night came and then morning,
but Farfallina didn't come down.
Marcel called to her, but she didn't answer.
He was very worried and terribly lonely.

Weeks went by.

The afternoons grew longer and warmer,

and Marcel went to the pond.

He was growing, and when he looked

at his reflection in the water,

he hardly **recognized** himself.

He went back to the tree every day to look
for Farfallina, but she was never there.
And after a while he gave up.
At the top of the tree Farfallina was **snuggled**
in a blanket of glossy silk.
She was growing too.

The sky was blue and clear the morning she was ready
to come out and open her beautiful new wings.

She had no idea how long she had been up in the tree,
and she floated down to find Marcel.

"I'll just wait," said Farfallina when she didn't see him,
and she sat on a flower.

Night came and then morning, but Marcel wasn't there.

Farfallina was tired and confused.

She **fluttered** around a bit and went to the pond.

 TEKS Make Inferences
Use details from the text to make an
inference about why Farfallina needs
to spend time alone in the tree.

The pond was glassy smooth
except for the ripples
made by a large, handsome goose
who was swimming in solitary circles.
Farfallina shivered with disappointment.

She went to the pond every day to look for the
small gray bird named Marcel, but he never came.
One morning the goose stopped his silent rounds
and spoke to her.

"You must like it here," he said.

Farfallina fluttered a bit.

"I've been waiting for a friend," she said sadly,

"but I don't think he'll come."

Marcel liked her smile and her brilliant colors.

"I know how you feel," he said. "I lost a friend too.

She just **vanished** into thin air."

Farfallina liked his sleek feathers and his gentle eyes.

"A ride around the pond might cheer you up,"

Marcel said.

Farfallina thought it would, and she settled

herself on Marcel's back.

"It's funny," Marcel said, "but I feel as though
I've known you a long time."
"I was just thinking the same thing," said Farfallina.
"My name is Farfallina. What's yours?"

Marcel stopped suddenly.

He beat the water with his strong wings.

Then he swam round and round and round.

"It's me Farfallina," he shouted. "It's me, Marcel!

Is that really you?"

"It is," Farfallina shouted back.

They looked at each other and laughed.

By evening they had explained everything,
and they fell asleep smiling at the stars.

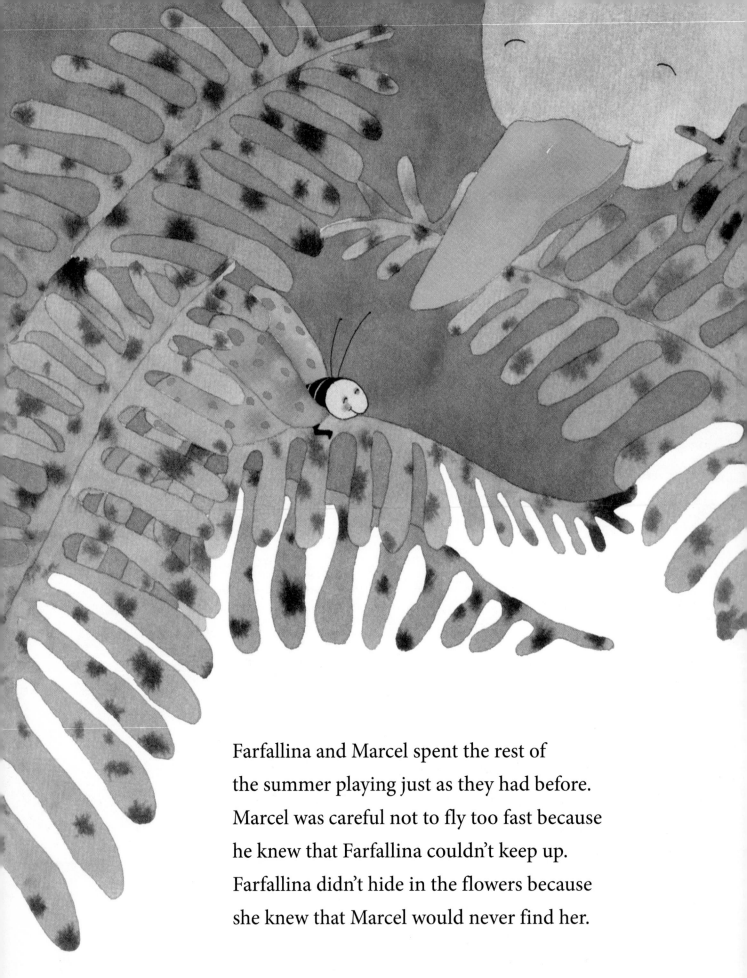

Farfallina and Marcel spent the rest of
the summer playing just as they had before.
Marcel was careful not to fly too fast because
he knew that Farfallina couldn't keep up.
Farfallina didn't hide in the flowers because
she knew that Marcel would never find her.

And when the leaves on the trees
around the pond turned red and gold,
they decided to go south.

Together.

Meet the Author

Holly Keller writes and illustrates books. Her ideas for books come from many places. The idea for *Farfallina and Marcel* started with the word *farfallina*. *Farfallina* means "little butterfly" in Italian. "For some reason," Holly says, "the word caught my fancy."

Other books written and illustrated by Holly Keller

LOG ON ▶ **FIND OUT**

Author Holly Keller
www.macmillanmh.com

Author's Purpose

Holly Keller tells a story about special friends. Write about two good friends. Tell what they do together and why they like each other.

278

✔ TEKS Comprehension Check

Retell the Story

Use the Retelling Cards to retell the story.

Retelling Cards

Think and Compare

1. What does Marcel like about Farfallina when they first meet? **Details**

2. Why did Farfallina and Marcel not recognize each other? **Character**

3. Why is Marcel lonely when Farfallina doesn't return? **Make Inferences**

4. What do you think the author wants readers to know about friendship? **Author's Purpose**

5. What is similar about the characters in "Leo Grows Up" on pages 254–255 and *Farfallina and Marcel*? **Reading/Writing Across Texts**

Genre
Expository text gives information and facts about a topic.

 Text Features
Illustrations are drawings that help readers to **clarify** and understand information.

Captions explain what is shown in the illustrations.

Content Vocabulary
patterns

stages

hatches

Monarch Butterfly

Butterflies

Butterflies come in all shapes and sizes. Some are big and some are small. Some have bright spots and some have other markings like dark **patterns** on their wings.

The Monarch and the Skipper are two kinds of butterflies. The Monarch is bigger and more colorful than the Skipper. The Monarch is bright orange and black. It has white spots. The Skipper is brown and has clear spots.

Although these two butterflies look different, they have the same body parts as all other butterflies.

Butterfly Body Parts

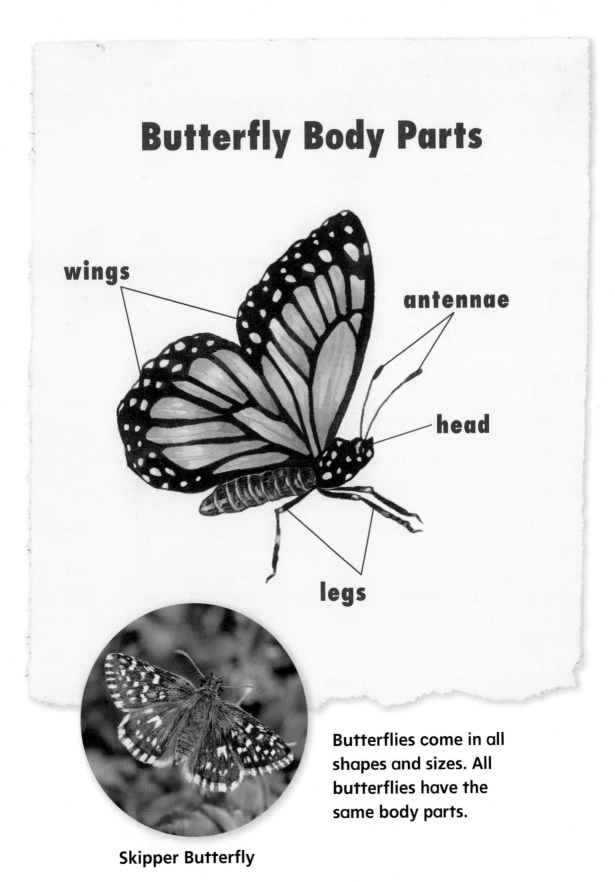

wings

antennae

head

legs

Skipper Butterfly

Butterflies come in all shapes and sizes. All butterflies have the same body parts.

281

How Butterflies Grow and Change

All butterflies become adults in the same way. Every butterfly's life has four steps, or **stages**, of development.

Stage 1: Egg

A butterfly begins life as an egg. The egg is about the size of the top of a pin. It is usually laid on a leaf. The egg is sticky, so it stays on the leaf.

Stage 2: Larva

When the egg **hatches**, a caterpillar comes out. This part of the butterfly's life is called the larva stage. When the caterpillar is large enough, it hooks itself onto a leaf or branch.

Stage 3: Pupa

The caterpillar makes a hard shell or case to live in. It usually stays inside the shell for a few weeks. This is called the pupa stage. Inside the shell the caterpillar grows and changes.

Stage 4: Adult

When the shell breaks open, the caterpillar has completely changed into a butterfly. This is the adult stage. After its wings are dry, the butterfly is ready to fly away.

 Connect and Compare

1. How do the illustrations help you **clarify** information about butterflies? What is the same about all butterflies? **Illustrations and Captions**

2. Use text from this selection and *Farfallina and Marcel* to help explain why Marcel does not know who Farfallina is. Use the names of at least two of the stages of a butterfly's life in your answer. **Reading/Writing Across Texts**

Science Activity

Use an encyclopedia to research two types of butterflies that live in your state.

LOG ON ▶ FIND OUT   **Science** Animal Growth
www.macmillanmh.com

Reading and Writing Connection

TEKS **Vary Words**

Good writers **vary the words** they use to make their writing more interesting.

I use different words to tell about the size of the puppy.

I vary the words here to tell more about how large the dog is.

22 SW 132 Place
Evanston, IL 60060
February 5, 2---

Dear Max,

It was nice to see you at my birthday party. My parents' gift was the best! The puppy they gave me has grown so much. He's huge! At first Murphy slept in my bed. Now he's so big and so heavy that he's sleeping on the floor. Even Murphy's snore is big!

See you soon!

Your friend,
Carlos

Your Writing Prompt

Having something new in your
life can be very fun!

Think about when you got
something new.

Write about this to a friend.

Writer's Checklist

✓ My writing is a letter that tells about
something new in my life.

☑ I **vary the words** that I use to make my
writing more interesting.

✓ I include details that give information
about what is new in my life.

✓ My spelling is correct. My sentences end
with the correct punctuation. I form
contractions correctly.

WILD ANIMALS

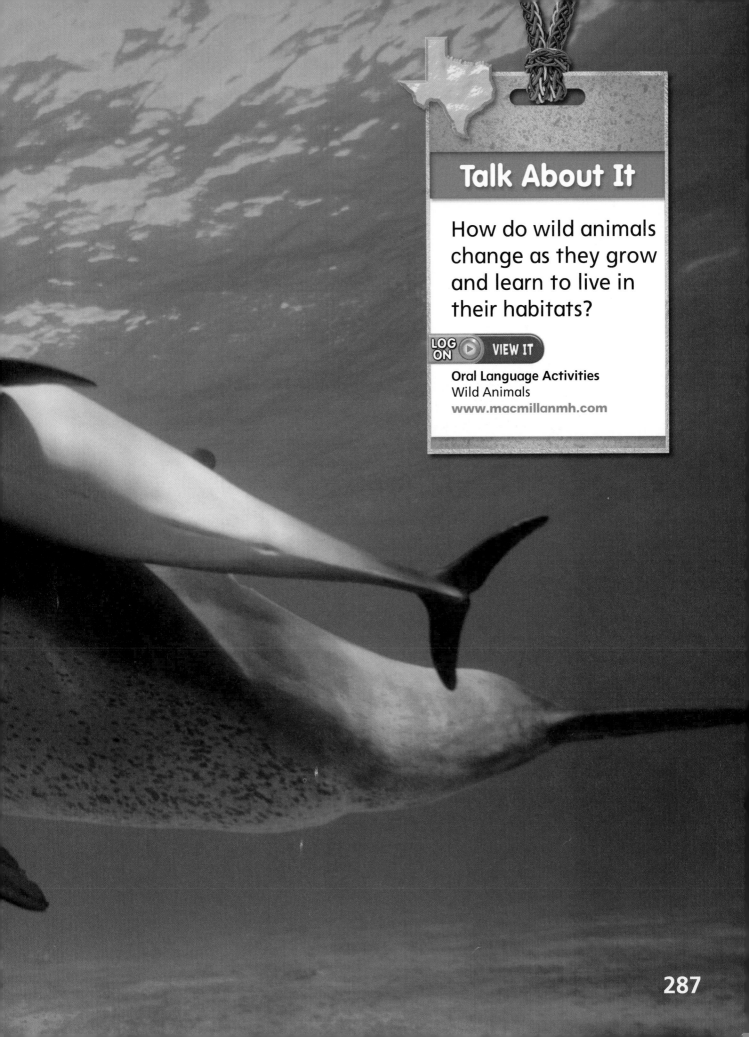

beloved
promised
wiggled
gleamed
glanced
noble

TEKS **Word Parts**

Word Endings added to the end of a verb can tell you when an event took place. The ending *-ed* shows that the action was in the past.

gleam + *ed* = *gleamed*

My Home in Alaska

May 15, 2–––

Dear Katie,

I am so happy to meet my new pen pal! I live in an Eskimo village in Alaska. I live with my parents and my **beloved** grandfather. I love him more than almost anybody!

I want to tell you about going with Grandpa to the tundra near my home. Grandpa had **promised** to show me a wolf. Last Sunday he kept his word.

We got up early. I put on my heavy sweater and **wiggled** into my boots. They were a tight fit so I moved my feet quickly from side to side to get them on.

Grandpa and I traveled by dog sled. The snow **gleamed** in the sun. It shone so brightly that we wore sunglasses. We stopped on a frozen lake. Grandpa **glanced** around, looking quickly in each direction. Then his eyes stopped. I looked at the same place. A wolf pack was near the lake. The **noble** wolves stood together. They looked impressive and as proud as kings. I will never forget those amazing animals.

Your new friend,

Jean

Reread for **Comprehension**

Adjust Reading Rate

TEKS **Make Inferences** Adjusting your reading rate by reading more slowly can help find clues to make inferences. Reread parts of the selection adjusting your reading rate. Use the chart to help make inferences about Jean.

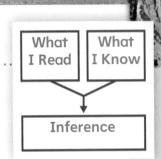

What I Read	What I Know

Inference

LOG ON ▶ LEARN IT · Comprehension
www.macmillanmh.com

289

Comprehension

Genre
Fiction is a story with made-up characters and events.

 Adjust Reading Rate

Make Inferences
As you read, use your Inference Chart.

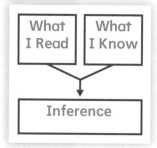

What I Read	What I Know

Inference

Read to Find Out
How do you know the boy and the wolf pup have a close friendship?

Nutik,
the Wolf Pup

by Jean Craighead George
illustrated by Ted Rand

Award
Winning
Author

In an Eskimo village at the top of the world lived a lively little boy. He was not very old, but he could run as fast as a bird's shadow.

When he ran, his father, Kapugen, the great hunter, caught him and lifted him high over his head.

When he ran, his mother, Ellen, caught him and hugged him closely.

When he ran, his big sister, Julie, caught him and carried him home to tell him wolf stories.

She told him how a wolf pack had saved her life when she was lost and starving on the vast tundra. The wolf pack's **noble** black leader had shared his family's food with her.

The wolf's name was Amaroq.

The little boy's name was Amaroq.

One day Julie came home with two pups. They were hungry and sickly. She put one in Amaroq's arms.

"Feed and tend this pup," she said. "His name is Nutik. I will feed and tend the other pup. I named her Uqaq. When they are fat and well, the wolves will come and get them."

Amaroq hugged his pup. He felt the little wolf heart beat softly. He kissed the warm head.

"Amaroq," Julie said when she saw this, "do not come to love this wolf pup. I have **promised** the wolves we will return the pups when they are fat and well."

Amaroq looked into Nutik's golden eyes. The wolf pup licked him and wagged his tail. Julie frowned.

"Don't fall in love, Amaroq," she warned again, "or your heart will break when the wolves come and take him away."

"No, it won't," he said.

TEKS Make Inferences

Use details from the story to make an inference about whether Amaroq will begin to love the wolf pup.

Julie gave Amaroq a bottle of milk to feed to his pup. Amaroq wrapped Nutik in soft rabbit skins, and they snuggled down on the grizzly-bear rug.

Every day Amaroq fed Nutik many bottles of milk, bites of raw meat, and bones to chew.

When the moon had changed from a crescent to a circle and back again, Nutik was fat. His legs did not wobble. His fur **gleamed**. He bounced and woofed. When Amaroq ran, Nutik ran.

Summer came to the top of the world. The sun stayed up all day and all night for three beautiful months.

Because of this, Amaroq and Nutik lived by a different clock.

They fell asleep to the gabble of baby snow geese. They awoke to the raspy hiss of snowy owlets.

They ate when they were hungry. They slept when they were tired, and they played wolf games in shadow and sun. They were never apart.

TEKS Locate Facts
Locating facts helps us understand the story. What does the sun do for three months in summer?

"Don't fall in love with Nutik," Julie warned again when the midnight sun was riding low. "I hear the wolves calling. Soon they will come for their pups." She looked at him. "Be strong."

"I am strong," he answered. "I am Amaroq."

One morning Amaroq and Nutik were tumbling on the mossy tundra when the wolf pack called. They were close by.

"Come home. Come home," they howled.

Nutik heard them.

Uqaq and Julie heard them.

Amaroq heard them. He got to his feet and ran.

Nutik stopped listening to the wolves and ran after him.

Amaroq led Nutik as fast as a falling star. He led him down a frost heave. He led him around the village schoolhouse. He led him far from the wolves.

After a long time he led Nutik home. Julie was at the door.

"Uqaq has returned to her family," she said. "The wolves came and got her. Nutik is next."

"I am very tired," Amaroq said, and he rubbed his eyes.

Julie put him to bed in his bearskin sleeping bag. When Julie tiptoed away, Nutik **wiggled** into the sleeping bag too. He licked Amaroq's cheek.

The sun set in August. The days grew shorter until there was no day at all. Now it was always nighttime.

In the blue grayness of the winter night the wolves came to the edge of the village.

When everyone was sleeping, they called to Nutik.

Nutik crawled out of Amaroq's sleeping bag and gently awakened him. He took his hand in his mouth and led him across the room. He stopped before Amaroq's parka. Amaroq put it on. Nutik picked up a boot. Amaroq put on his boots.

Nutik whimpered at the door.

Amaroq opened it. They stepped into the cold.

The wolves were prancing and dancing like ice spirits on the hill.

Nutik took Amaroq's mittened hand and led him toward his wolf family. The frost crackled under their feet. The wolves whispered their welcome.

Suddenly Amaroq stopped. Nutik was taking him to his wolf home.

"No, Nutik," he said. "I cannot go with you. I cannot live with your family." Nutik tilted his head to one side and whimpered, "Come."

"You must go home alone," Amaroq said, and hugged his **beloved** wolf pup for a long time.

Then he turned and walked away. He did not run. Nutik did not chase him.

"I am very strong," Amaroq said to himself.

He got home before his tears froze.

Amaroq crawled into his bearskin sleeping bag and sobbed. His heart was broken after all.

At last he fell asleep.

Julie awoke him for breakfast.

"I don't want to eat," he told her. "Last night the wolves came and took Nutik away."

"You are a strong boy," she said. "You let him go back to his family. That is right."

TEKS **Make Inferences**
Use evidence from the text to make an inference about why Amaroq let Nutik return to his family.

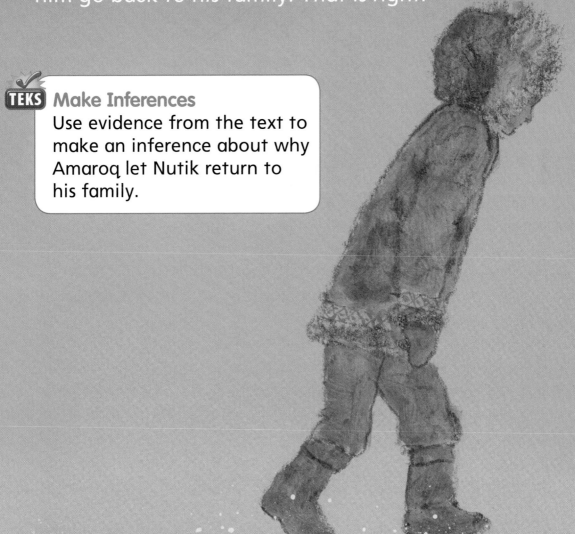

307

Amaroq did not eat lunch. When Kapugen took him out to fish, he did not fish. Tears kept welling up. He ran home to hide them in his bearskin sleeping bag.

It was surprisingly warm.

Up from the bottom and into Amaroq's arms wiggled the furry wolf pup.

"Nutik," Amaroq cried joyfully. He hugged his friend and **glanced** at Julie. Instead of scolding him, she stepped outside.

"Dear wolves," she called across the tundra. "Your beautiful pup, Nutik, will not be coming back to you. He has joined our family.

"Amaroq loves Nutik. Nutik loves Amaroq. They are brothers now. He cannot leave."

As if listening, the wind stopped blowing. In the stillness Julie called out clearly and softly:

"I shall take care of him as lovingly as you took care of me."

And the wolves sang back, "That is good."

Meet the
Author and Illustrator

Jean Craighead George has written more than 100 children's books.

One summer Jean went to Alaska to learn more about wolves. There she saw a little girl walking on the lonely tundra. She also saw a beautiful male wolf. They became the characters for Jean's book *Julie of the Wolves*, for older readers. *Nutik, the Wolf Pup* is a follow-up to that book.

To draw the illustrations for *Nutik, the Wolf Pup*, **Ted Rand** went to Alaska. He wanted to see the tundra for himself. Ted has illustrated more than 60 children's books.

LOG ON ▶ **FIND OUT**

Author Jean Craighead George
Illustrator Ted Rand
www.macmillanmh.com

Other books written by Jean Craighead George

Author's Purpose

Jean Craighead George tells a story about a boy and a wolf pup in an Eskimo village. Write about what living in a village like Amaroq's might be like.

✔ TEKS Comprehension Check

Retell the Story

Use the Retelling Cards to retell the story.

Retelling Cards

Think and Compare

1. Who cared for Julie when she was lost and starving? Details

2. What happened when Nutik went back to the wolf pack? Cause and Effect

3. Why does Julie let Nutik stay with Amaroq at the end of the story? Make Inferences

4. What does the author want readers to know about Amaroq and Nutik's friendship? Author's Purpose

5. Do you think Jean in "My Home in Alaska," on pages 288–289, and Amaroq might be friends? What are some things that they have in common? Reading/Writing Across Texts

What I Read	What I Know

Inference

WOLVES

Wolves are wild animals that are related to the dog family. They look similar to dogs, but they have longer legs and larger feet. They also have more powerful jaws.

Wolves live in different areas, or **habitats**. Some wolves are gray. Others are almost black. Wolves that live in northern Alaska are white. All wolves have long, bushy tails.

Habitat

Wolves live in forest or mountain habitats. Wolves need lots of land because they move around a lot. They **roam**, or travel, 20 miles a day to look for and find food.

Wolves are endangered animals. They used to live all over North America, but now they live only in northern forests and Alaska.

Food

Wolves are hunters. They have a good sense of smell. This helps them find their **prey**. Wolves that live in forests eat mice, rabbits, deer, and moose. Wolves in Alaska also eat caribou or oxen. Finding food is not easy for wolves. Sometimes they must follow a herd for several days. They swallow food in large pieces without chewing. Wolves can eat 20 pounds of meat at one time.

Life Cycle

The female wolf gives birth to pups in the spring. First she finds or digs a den. Often she will use the same den year after year. The cubs cannot see or hear when they are born. Their mother stays with them for about three weeks. During this time the male brings food for the mother to eat.

After about a month, the pups can eat meat. All of the pack members hunt food for them. The female hunts, too. Another pack member takes care of the pups while she is away. By fall the pups have learned to hunt. They are ready to travel with the pack.

Encyclopedia entries often have words in dark print called headings. These summarize what the following section will be about.

The Pack

Wolves live in family groups called packs. A pack may have 7 or 8 wolves. One male is the leader of the pack. He has a female mate. Their children are part of the pack, too. A pack may also have an aunt or an uncle.

 ## Connect and Compare

1. In which section would you find information about where wolves live? What did you learn about in the section with the heading "Food"? **Headings**

2. Think about the encyclopedia entry and *Nutik, the Wolf Pup*. How would Nutik's life have been different if he had never left his pack? **Reading/Writing Across Texts**

Science Activity

Research a type of wolf. Write facts about what the wolf looks like and where it lives. Share with your class. Remember to speak clearly at an appropriate pace.

LOG ON ▶ FIND OUT Science Wolves
www.macmillanmh.com

TEKS A Strong Conclusion

A good writer includes a **strong concluding sentence** at the end of a piece of writing.

Reading and Writing Connection

My concluding sentence wraps up my report.

I state the title one final time.

My Book Report
by Jan O.

I really liked <u>Animals of the Sea and Shore</u> by Ann O. Squire. The book describes many animals that live in or near the ocean. Some animals, like whales, live in the water. Other animals live on shore, like snails.

I also learned some unusual facts. Did you know that sea otters sleep floating on their backs? If you like learning about the creatures that live by the water, you'll like <u>Animals of the Sea and Shore.</u>

Your Writing Prompt

A book report gives information about a book.

Think about a book that you have read about animals.

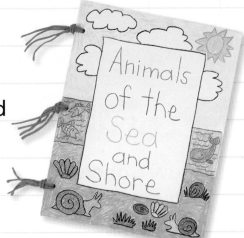

Write a book report about this book. Describe why you liked or disliked it.

Writer's Checklist

✓ My book report clearly gives information about a book about animals that I have read.

✓ I include a **strong concluding sentence** to complete my book report.

✓ I include details that give the reader specific information about my book.

✓ My spelling is correct. My sentences are complete. The pronouns and verbs in my writing agree in number.

Review

Draw Conclusions
Sequence of Events
Summarize
Diagrams and Labels
Homophones

A Birthday Treat

Mom   Dad   Jessie

Jessie's friends

Mom: We are going to the science museum for your birthday today!

Jessie: Hooray! That's my favorite place! Can I invite my friends Ashley, Samantha, and Blake to go with me, please?

Mom: I'm sorry, but I have only two tickets. Also, we need to leave right away. We don't want to miss the volcano movie. Fasten your seat belt. Do you remember where the museum is?

Jessie: Yes. Make a left onto Elm Street. Make a right at the gas station onto Pine Street. The museum is on the right.

Mom: We have 45 minutes before the movie starts. Do you want to look around?

Jessie: Sure! Let's check out the dinosaur exhibit. The dinosaur skeletons reach to the ceiling!

Mom: Before we go, I need to stop at the cafeteria. Let's open the door.

Jessie: What's this?

Jessie's friends: Surprise! Happy birthday!

Mom and Dad: Surprise!

Jessie: Wow! What a great birthday treat!

The Invention of Hook-and-Loop Tape

Did you ever wonder how inventors come up with their ideas? Do they study something closely? Do they work with partners? Or do ideas come to them by accident?

Inventions may begin in any of these ways. Or they may be the result of them all. That's how it happened for George de Mestral. His invention is hook-and-loop tape. That is the sticky fabric tape that fastens sneakers, caps, and backpacks.

The prickly bur is a seedpod of the burdock plant.

George's idea began when he returned from a walk with his dog. Burs were stuck to his pants and his dog's fur. George pulled them off, but wondered how they held on.

George began to study the burs. What if he could discover the secret of their strong grip? Maybe he could invent a strong fastener.

George's breakthrough came with a microscope. He saw that burs were covered with tiny hooks. The hooks grabbed onto anything with a loop!

Next George worked with a weaver to make one piece of tape with hooks and another piece with loops. Put together, the pieces imitated a bur.

Today people use hook-and-loop tape instead of buttons, strings, or zippers.

hook

loop

The hooks attach to the loops in the same way burs grab tightly to fur.

Comprehension

Poetry

- Rhyme, rhythm, and repetition help to create images in poetry.

- Review the poem "The Puppy" on page 116.

- Identify which words in this poem rhyme and give it a rhythm.

- Then, in a small group, discuss how the words used in this poem help you picture what taking care of a puppy might be like.

Writing

Write a Poem

- Think about your favorite animal. Write a poem that describes how it looks, what it feels and sounds like, and where it lives. Include words that rhyme or create a rhythm.

Word Study

Phonics

Open and Closed Syllables

- Review the words *tiger*, *publish*, *lazy*, *human*, *second*, and *happen*. With a partner, say each word aloud and identify the open or closed syllables. Then use each word in an oral sentence.

Spelling

Words with Open and Closed Syllables

- Review this week's spelling words then read the paragraph below. Identify spelling words with open and closed syllables. List the words on a separate piece of paper.

My family and I live in a giant log cabin. When my friends come for a visit, we play baseball out in the open field. Sometimes we see baby animals. It is always fun and crazy at our cabin.

The Big Question

How do we learn about nature?

Theme Video Nature
www.macmillanmh.com

How do we learn about nature?

Observing plants and animals helps us learn how they live in different environments. We notice how habitats are different and what animals and plants do to meet their needs in different places. People also use natural resources from the environment. Wood from trees is used to make pencils, water from rivers is used to grow fruits and vegetables, and coal mined from the earth is used as fuel. Learning about these natural resources will help you to preserve the environment so living things have what they need to survive.

Research Activities

Throughout this unit you will gather information. As a class, we will make a list of natural resources and the environment topics, along with open-ended questions. Choose one topic to focus on and create a nonfiction picture book that describes your topic.

Keep Track of Ideas

As you read, keep track of all you learn about the world and its natural resources. Use the **Layered Book Foldable**. On the top flap, write the unit theme. On each layer of the book, write the weekly theme. Inside each layer, write facts you learn each week.

The World Around Us

Plant and Animal Habitats

Animal Needs

Protecting Earth

Weather Facts

Nature Stories

Digital Learning

Interactive Student Book

- **Research Roadmap**
  Follow a step-by-step guide to complete your research project.

Texas Online Resources

- Topic Finder and Other Research Tools
- Videos and Virtual Field Trips
- Photos and Drawings for Presentations
- Related Articles and Web Resources
- Texas Web Site Links

Lady Bird Johnson Wildflower Center

The former First Lady and the actress Helen Hayes started this garden to showcase the landscapes and ecological heritage of Texas.

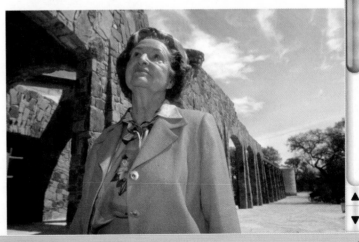

Plant and Animal Habitats

Talk About It

Think about life in the desert. What do plants and animals need to live there?

LOG ON ▶ VIEW IT

Oral Language Activities
Habitats
www.macmillanmh.com

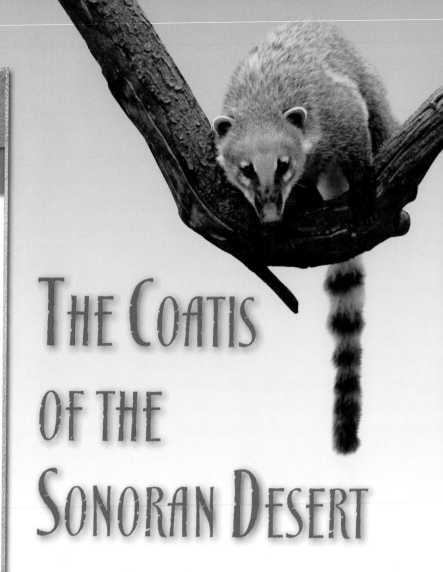

Vocabulary

burrow
beyond
warning
lengthy
distant

TEKS Content Clues

A **possessive noun** shows ownership. An apostrophe (') and *s* are added to a singular noun to make it possessive.

The *ranger's* map fits in his pocket.

The map belongs to the ranger.

THE COATIS OF THE SONORAN DESERT

by Nya Taylor

Coatis (ko-WAH-tees) are animals that live in the desert. They look like raccoons and are about as big as cats. They have long tails that help them balance as they climb.

Coatis like to eat plants and insects. They use their claws to dig for small animals that may be living underground in a **burrow**. Some coatis eat while hanging from trees.

Coatis live together. They do not wander **beyond** their group. Staying close together helps them hear **warning** calls if danger is near. Coatis spend hours taking **lengthy** rests in the shade. During the hot days, they need to stay cool. At night they climb into trees to sleep.

You can see coatis at the Sonora Desert Museum in Arizona. The park has workers to help you. You may ask to use a ranger's binoculars to see far away. The binoculars will help you spot coatis in the trees in the **distant** mountains.

Reread for **Comprehension**

Ask Questions

TEKS **Author's Purpose** Asking questions as you read is one way to **clarify** information in a text. Asking questions can help you understand the author's purpose for writing a text. Authors write to inform, entertain, persuade, or inquire. Reread the text and use the chart to help generate questions and identify clues that will help you identify the author's purpose.

Clue	Clue

Author's Purpose

LOG ON ▶ LEARN IT Comprehension
www.macmillanmh.com

331

Comprehension

Genre
Fiction is a made-up story that may give facts about a real topic.

Ask Questions
TEKS **Author's Purpose**
As you read, use your Author's Purpose Chart.

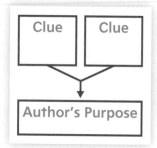

Read to Find Out
What do you learn about the toad?

332

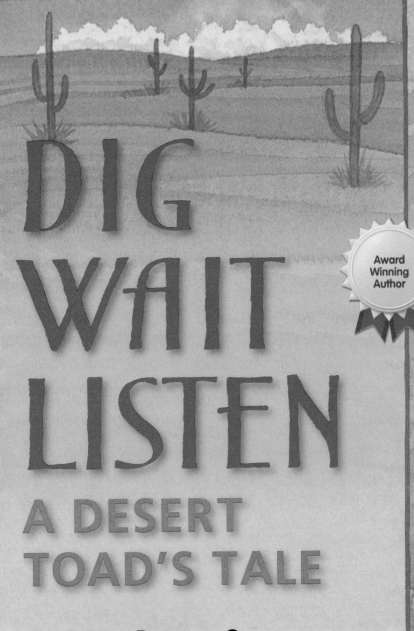

DIG WAIT LISTEN
A DESERT TOAD'S TALE

by April Pulley Sayre

Illustrated by Barbara Bash

Award Winning Author

Deep in the desert,
under the sand, the spadefoot
toad waits. She waits...for the
sound of rain.

Skitter, skitter, scratch.
She hears soft sounds.
Is this the rain at last?

No. It's the scorpion overhead,
crawling slowly past.
Skitter, scratch!

Thunk, thunk, thunk.
Clink, clunk,
clink, clunk.
Sounds shake the soil.

But it's only a herd of peccaries.
Their hooves hammer the ground.

Pop, pop, pop.
What's that sound now?
Is this the rain at last?

No, it's a rat,
hopping in **lengthy** leaps
like a tiny kangaroo.

Will the rain *ever* come?
The desert's so hot, so dry!
And the toad's been waiting
so many months in her
basement **burrow** home.

TEKS **Author's Purpose**
Why does the author include information
about other desert animals?

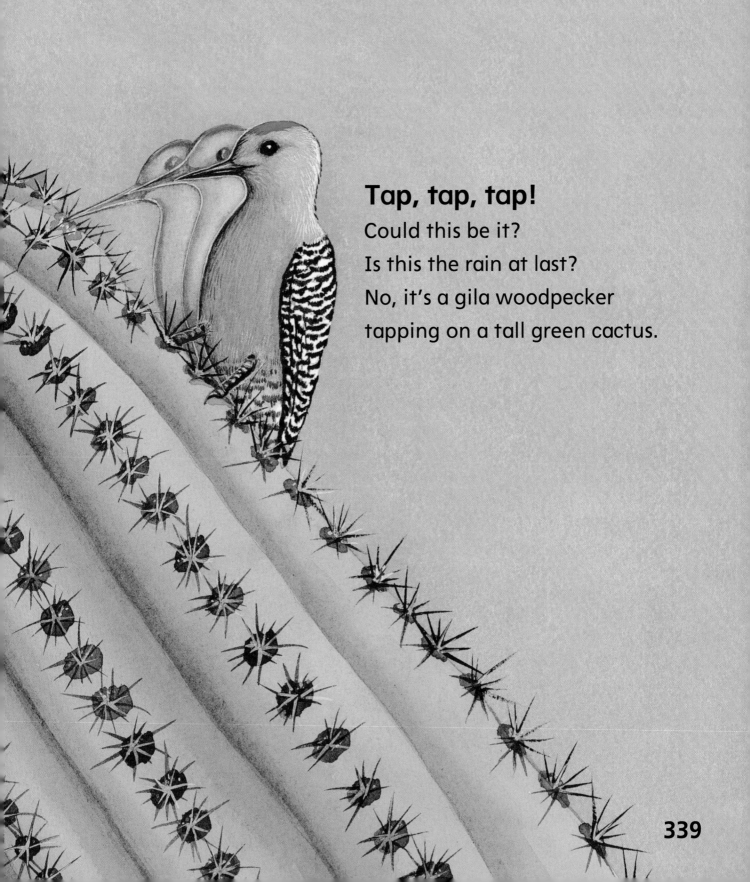

Tap, tap, tap!

Could this be it?

Is this the rain at last?

No, it's a gila woodpecker

tapping on a tall green cactus.

The toad feels the ground begin to shake.
Then a **crunch, crunch, crunch**
that's loud.
Is this the rain?

No. It's a park ranger's boots
walking on the path.

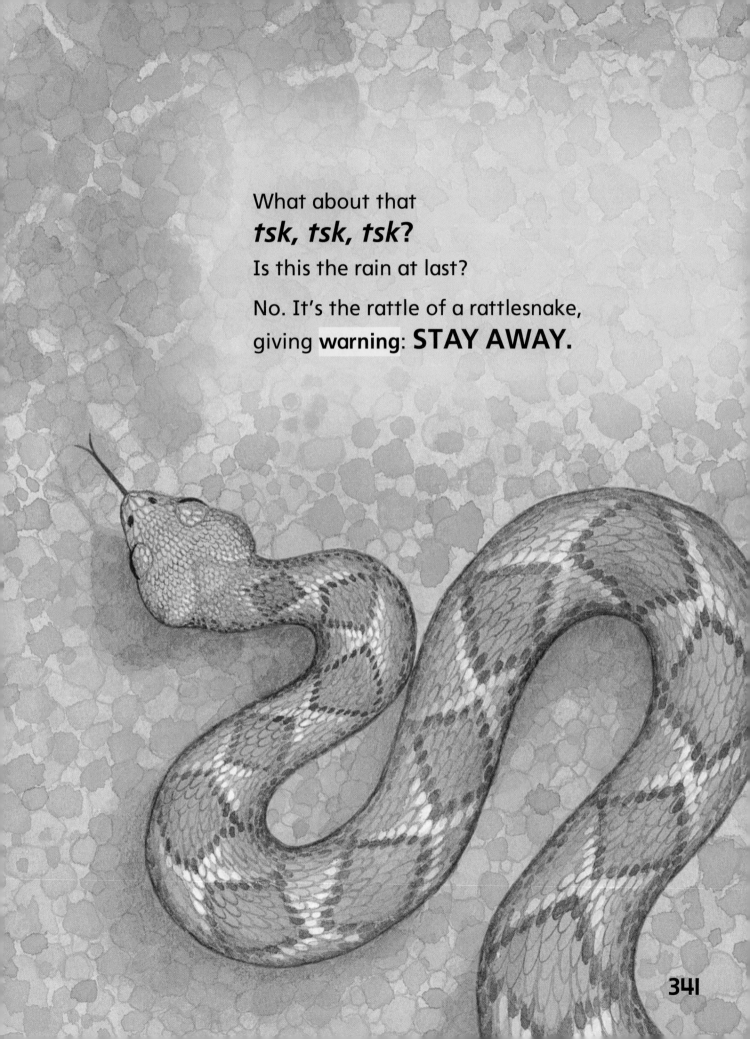

What about that
tsk, tsk, tsk?

Is this the rain at last?

No. It's the rattle of a rattlesnake,
giving warning: STAY AWAY.

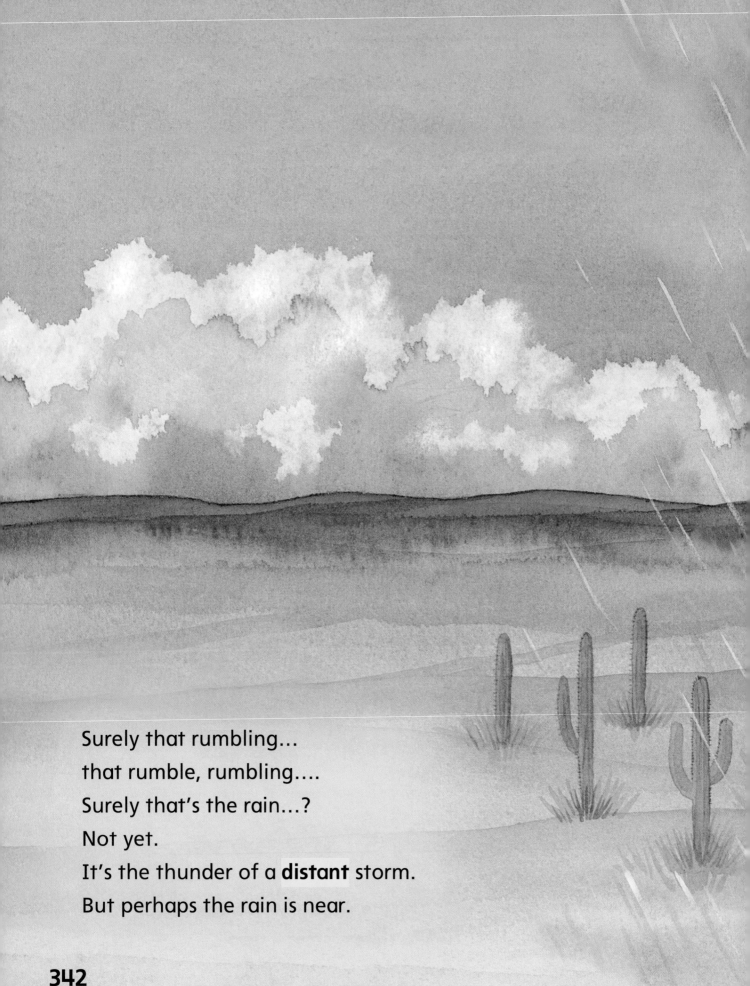

Surely that rumbling...
that rumble, rumbling....
Surely that's the rain...?
Not yet.
It's the thunder of a **distant** storm.
But perhaps the rain is near.

342

Plip, plop, **plip,** plop.
Plip, plop, **plop!**
Is this the rain at last?
Plop **thunk.** Plop **thunk.**
Plop **thunk** *gussssshhhhhhh!*

It is rain!

The toad hears it.

She digs.

Plop thunk.
Plop thunk.
Plop thunk *gusssssshhhhhh!*
Heavy rain pounds the desert floor.

Push, push, and the toad pops right out, into
the open air.

Bleat, bleat, bleat!
The toad hears loud bleats.
Is that the rain sound too?

No. It's male spadefoot toads,
calling: Here, come here!

Plop **thunk.** Plop **thunk.** Plop **thunk** *gusssssshhhhhhh!*
The toad hops in a puddle.
She lays her eggs,
like beads of glass.

345

Plop **thunk**, plop **thunk**, plop **thunk**
gusssssshhhhhhh!

Two days later, the eggs hatch. Wriggling and wiggling in their puddle home, the tadpoles are here at last!

They eat.

They grow.

Legs start to show.

But their puddle is drying up!

Will any make it?

Yes!
With new legs formed,
young toads crawl
from their puddle home.
They rest, then

into the desert **beyond**.

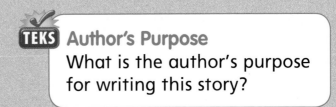

TEKS Author's Purpose
What is the author's purpose
for writing this story?

Thump, thump, thump.

Hundreds of tiny toads jump.

The rain has made the desert green.

TEKS Asking Questions

What questions can you ask about the noise described on this page?

Yet it won't be long till the desert's dry,
and toads dig down deep with their
spadefoot feet, to wait for that sound...
that marvelous sound,
the sound of the desert rain.

Plop **thunk**, plop **thunk**,

plop **thunk** *gusssssshhhhhhh!*

Plop **thunk**, plop **thunk**,

plop **thunk** *gusssssshhhhhhh!*

Plop **thunk**, plop **thunk**,

plop **thunk** *gusssssshhhhhhhh!*

ENJOY THE OUTDOORS WITH APRIL AND BARBARA

"I love writing—most of the time," says author **April Pulley Sayre**. "Sometimes my first try is horrible. But I rewrite until I like every paragraph. I try to communicate the excitement I feel about nature."

A love of nature also drives artist **Barbara Bash**. When she does research, she uses books and photos to get to know the topic. Next, Barbara visits the places in the stories. "Then," she says, "something alive and personal can be expressed through my books."

LOG ON ▶ FIND OUT

Author April Pulley Sayre
Illustrator Barbara Bash
www.macmillanmh.com

Other books written and illustrated by Barbara Bash

Author's Purpose
April Pulley Sayre teaches readers about desert toads. Think about an animal you know. Write about its life cycle or how it grows and changes in its habitat.

TEKS Comprehension Check

Retell the Story

Use the Retelling Cards to retell the story.

Retelling Cards

Think and Compare

1. Where does the desert toad wait for the rain? **Details**

2. What happens after it finally begins to rain in the desert? **Sequence of Events**

3. Why might it be difficult for some animals to live in the desert? **Make Inferences**

4. Why did the author write about the desert toad? **Author's Purpose**

5. How are the coatis in "The Coatis of the Sonoran Desert," on pages 330–331, and the spadefoot toad in *Dig, Wait, Listen* different? How are they alike? **Reading/Writing Across Texts**

Clue	Clue

↓

Author's Purpose

The Sonoran Desert

The Sonoran Desert is a dry area in the American Southwest. It covers about 100,000 square miles in parts of California, Arizona, and Mexico. Some parts of the Sonoran Desert may not have rain for one or two years. Other parts have sudden summer rainstorms more frequently.

Summer in the Sonoran Desert is very, very hot. The **temperature** is often more than 100 degrees during the day. Even in the winter, the temperature is usually above freezing.

Desert plants and animals have **adapted** to life in the desert. They have special ways to survive with very little water and in very hot weather.

Plants

The Sonoran Desert has many different kinds of cactus plants. Cactus plants can live a long time without rain.

Cactus plants store water in their thick stems. They also have thick, waxy leaves that help keep in water. Cactus roots grow close to the top of the ground. When it does rain, the roots can soak up the water very quickly.

Sonoran Desert Animals

Name	Type of Animal	What It Eats
black-chinned hummingbird	bird	flowers, nectar, nuts
coyote	mammal	small animals, insects, plants
ground snake	reptile	insects
horned toad	reptile	plants, insects
roadrunner	bird	insects, lizards, snakes
Sonoran Desert toad	amphibian	insects, mice

The animal name is in the first column.

Information about the animal is in the row.

Animals

Like desert plants, desert animals can live without much rain. Most desert animals do not have to drink water. They get the water they need from their food.

Many desert animals are **nocturnal**. This means they come out to find food only at night, when it is cool. During the hot days, these animals hide in the shade or underground. Staying cool helps animals keep water in their bodies.

 Connect and Compare

1. Which desert animals eat insects? Which desert animals eat only plants? **Chart**

2. Think about this encyclopedia article and *Dig, Wait, Listen*. How is the spadefoot toad like the other animals of the Sonoran Desert? **Reading/Writing Across Texts**

Science Activity

Use an encyclopedia or other references to research desert plants. Make a chart that gives two facts for each plant.

LOG ON ▶ FIND OUT **Science** Desert Facts
www.macmillanmh.com

Reading and Writing Connection

TEKS **Important Details**

Good writers use **important details** in their writing. Details tell more about the writer's main idea.

This detail describes the desert heat.

This detail tells the reader how the cactus looks.

June 1, 2---

Dear Cheryl,

How is your summer? Mine has been fantastic so far!

Last weekend, my dad took me to a desert. The air was so hot that it shimmered. The ground was so dry that there were cracks in it! The most amazing thing I saw was a cactus. The cactus was ten feet tall and covered with hundreds of spines. My dad and I had a terrific time.

I will send you pictures soon.

Sincerely,

Maria

Your Writing Prompt

Animals live in amazing places, such as deserts and rain forests.

Think about a plant or animal habitat that you have studied.

Write a letter to a friend that describes this habitat.

Writer's Checklist

✓ My writing is a letter that clearly describes a plant or animal habitat.

✓ My ideas are grouped together in a way that makes sense and is easy for readers to understand.

☑ There are important details that describe what the habitat looks and sounds like.

✓ My spelling and punctuation are correct. I use interesting adjectives to describe nouns.

Animal Needs

363

Animals Need to Eat

by Patty Serrano

Vocabulary

beasts
puddles
nibble
itches
preen
handy

TEKS Word Parts
The word endings –s and –es can be added to make nouns plural.

beast + s = beasts

Many *beasts* live at the zoo.

Alphabetize
Put the words above in alphabetical order. Check the Glossary to see if they are correct.

All animals need to eat, but different **beasts** eat in different ways.

A raccoon searches for fish, nuts, and other things to eat. Raccoons wash all their food before eating it. To do this, they must live near water. Even small pools of water, like **puddles**, will do. After the raccoon washes its food, it begins to eat by taking small bites. The animal may **nibble** on an acorn once it is clean.

A tiger hunts for the meat it eats. Eating can make a mess out of the tiger's fur. There are many places that need to be scratched. To get rid of these **itches**, the tiger bathes in a pond. Later the tiger may lie in the sun and **preen**. It carefully smooths its fur with its tongue.

A spider eats meat, too. It builds a sticky web and then hides. The web is a useful tool for the spider. Bugs get stuck in the **handy** web. Then the spider's dinner cannot escape.

Reread for Comprehension

Animal	Animal	Animal
Behavior	Behavior	Behavior

Ask Questions

Compare and Contrast To compare means to tell how things are alike. To contrast means to tell how they are different. Asking questions about what is the same or different can help you compare and contrast information in an article. Use the chart to compare and contrast how the animals in this selection get food.

Comprehension

Genre
Expository selections use photographs and captions to tell about a topic.

Ask Questions
Compare and Contrast
As you read, use your Compare and Contrast Chart.

Animal	Animal	Animal
Behavior	Behavior	Behavior

Read to Find Out
How do the different animals keep themselves clean?

Splish! Splash!
ANIMAL BATHS

Award Winning Author

by APRIL PULLEY SAYRE

SPLISH! SPLASH!

Take a bath.

Brush your
teeth clean.

And think of
the animals.

They clean
themselves, too.

Squirt!

An elephant sprays
water over its back.

Squirt!!

Baby will get a
shower, too.

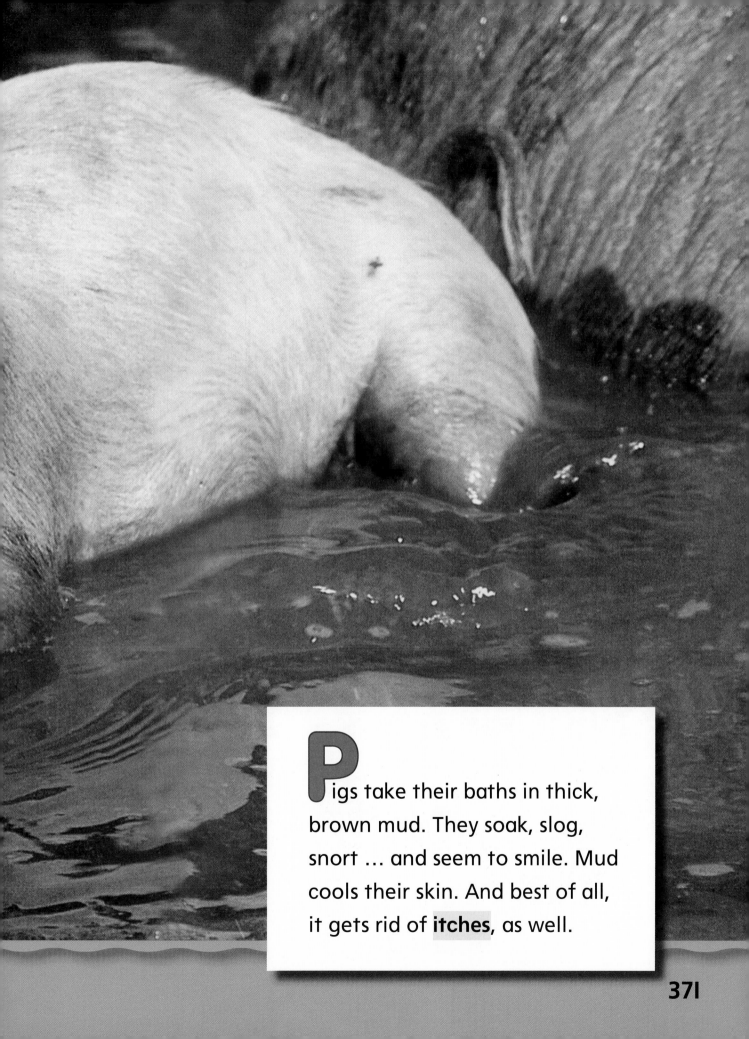

Pigs take their baths in thick, brown mud. They soak, slog, snort … and seem to smile. Mud cools their skin. And best of all, it gets rid of **itches**, as well.

Birds take baths in **puddles**. Or shower under sprinklers or waterfalls.

Once clean, they **preen**—
smoothing, fluffing, and
straightening their feathers.
That's like hair brushing for you.

 TEKS **Compare and Contrast**
How does the way a bird takes a bath
differ from the way a pig does?

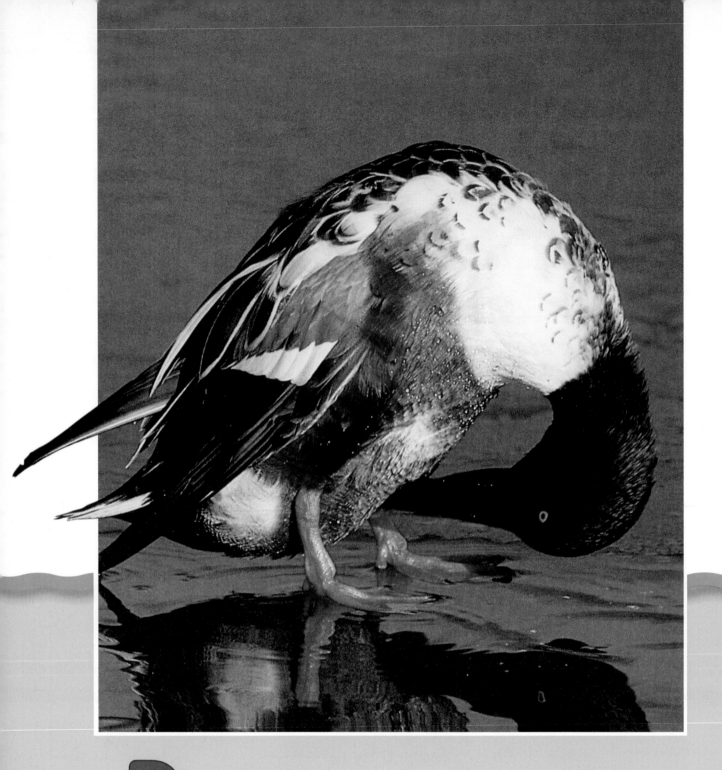

Ducks do extra work. They spread oil on their feathers. This special oil waterproofs them. Without it, ducks would get soggy and cold … which wouldn't be *ducky* at all!

Bears have long fur that gets itchy and full of insects.
To scratch itches, a bear rubs against a tree.
Bears also take dust baths. They roll in dirt.
Or they swim and splash in a wide, cool stream.

Even the king of **beasts** can get beastly dirty. So lions do what house cats do. They lick their long fur clean. But even a lion's tongue can't reach the back of its head ... so it licks a paw and rubs it over its head and ears.

376

A comb might come in **handy** for cleaning a chimpanzee's fur. But chimps don't have combs, so fingers work fine.

Chimps bite and pull bugs and leaves
from their family's and friends' fur.
What are good buddies for?

379

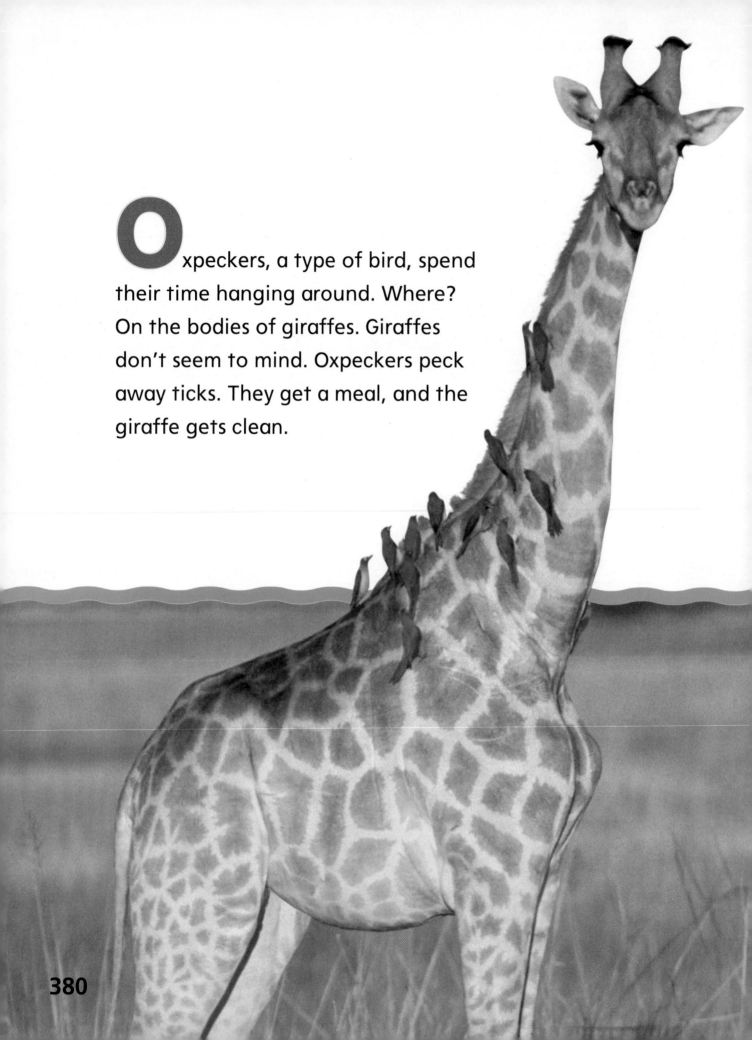

Oxpeckers, a type of bird, spend their time hanging around. Where? On the bodies of giraffes. Giraffes don't seem to mind. Oxpeckers peck away ticks. They get a meal, and the giraffe gets clean.

Hippos have helpers, too. But these helpers are under water, in the rivers and ponds where hippos wade. Fish **nibble** algae off a hippo's skin. Does it tickle the hippo? Only hippos know. And they won't say.

Fish don't take baths. They live in water. But some do try to stay clean. Big fish wait in line—not for a car wash, but for a cleaner fish.

Nibble, nibble, the cleaner fish bites tiny pests off the big fish's scales. The big fish gets clean. The cleaner fish gets a meal. Now that's an amazing deal!

 TEKS **Compare and Contrast**
Name some ways animals help each other stay clean. How are they alike? How are they different?

Nearby, a shrimp crawls into a moray eel's mouth.

Will it become a shrimp dinner? Not this time. It's a cleaner shrimp— an animal dentist.

It picks and eats food off the moray's teeth. Instead of being a shrimp dinner, it's dinnertime for this shrimp!

TEKS **Asking Questions**
What questions can you ask about how eels keep clean?

Now that you've heard
about animal baths and animal
dentists, and how animals splish,
splash, peck, and preen ...
it's time to take *your* bath.

Splish and splash.

And think of the animals.
They, too, are getting clean.

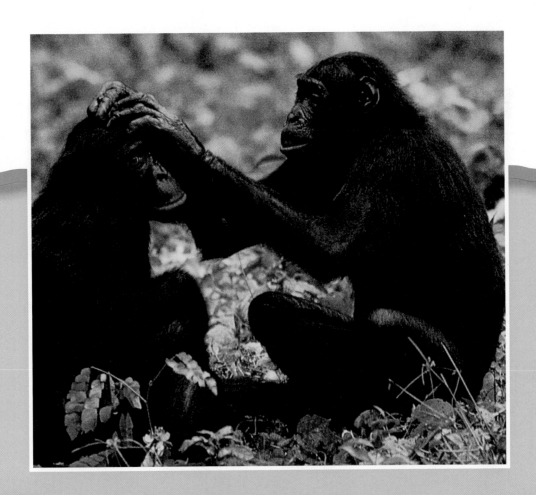

Splish! Splash!
April Has Fun on the Job

April Pulley Sayre has written more than 50 books. Many of them are about plants and animals.

"As a child," April says, "I spent hours picking flowers, watching insects, reading books, and writing. Now I do the same thing, only as a career." April's favorite part of the work is researching. She likes reading books and magazines, calling people, and visiting museums, parks, and wild places.

Other books written by April Pulley Sayre

LOG ON ▶ **FIND OUT**
Author April Pulley Sayre
www.macmillanmh.com

🖊 TEKS Author's Purpose

The author explains how animals get clean. Describe what you do to keep clean.

TEKS Comprehension Check

Retell the Selection

Use the Retelling Cards to retell the selection.

Retelling Cards

Think and Compare

1. Where do Oxpeckers like to spend time? Details

2. Use details from the text to compare and contrast how lions and chimps keep themselves clean. Compare and Contrast

Animal	Animal	Animal
Behavior	Behavior	Behavior

3. Which animal bathes in the most unusual way? Main Idea and Details

4. The author explains how each animal keeps clean. What do you think she wants readers to learn? Author's Purpose

5. How is "Animals Need to Eat" on pages 364–365 like *Splish! Splash!*? How is it different? Reading/Writing Across Texts

389

Ant and Grasshopper

based on Aesop's Fable

Characters: Narrator, Ant, Grasshopper

Setting: a meadow with an anthill in the summer.

Scene 1

Narrator: It was summer in the meadow. Most of the insects were working hard to gather food.

Grasshopper: What a beautiful summer day! Ant, why are you working so hard? Come play leaf hop with me!

Ant: I am putting away food for winter so I will not be hungry. I don't have time for playing games.

Grasshopper: Winter is so far away. You have plenty of time!

Ant: Winter lasts as long as summer. You have to be ready! I think you should save some food.

Grasshopper: I'll do it next week. There is no rush.

Narrator: Week after week, Ant worked. Week after week, Grasshopper played leaf hop.

Scene 2

Narrator: Soon winter came. The meadow was covered with snow. There was no food to be found.

Grasshopper: Ant, please help me. I am cold and hungry.

Ant: Oh, Grasshopper, you did not plan. I will give you some food, but next summer you must gather food for yourself.

Narrator: Ant gave Grasshopper some food. Ant also taught Grasshopper an important lesson!

TEKS Connect and Compare

1. Why is the setting of the play important to the characters' feelings and actions? **Setting**

2. Think about this play and the selection *Splish! Splash!* How do the animals in both selections get what they need? **Reading/Writing Across Texts**

TEKS **Strong Topic Sentence**

Remember to write a strong **topic sentence** for each paragraph. A topic sentence tells exactly what the paragraph is about.

① Notes

Chimpanzees, Africa,

② Notes

rocks
sticks

③ Notes

take leaves off the sticks, poke sticks in termite hill, eat insects off stick

Chimps Need Tools

by Jewel W.

Chimps need simple tools to get food. A tool can be something from nature. In Africa, chimps use rocks to crack open nuts. Other chimps use sticks to get and eat termites from termite hills.

The paragraph begins with a topic sentence.

This sentence supports my topic sentence.

392

Your Writing Prompt

All animals have needs.

Think about animals that you know about. Find out facts about one animal's needs.

Now, write a summary about that animal's needs.

Writer's Checklist

✓ My writing is clearly about animal needs.

☑ My summary starts with a strong topic sentence.

✓ I include sentences with details that support my topic sentence.

✓ The punctuation in my sentences is correct. I use the words *a* and *an* in the right places.

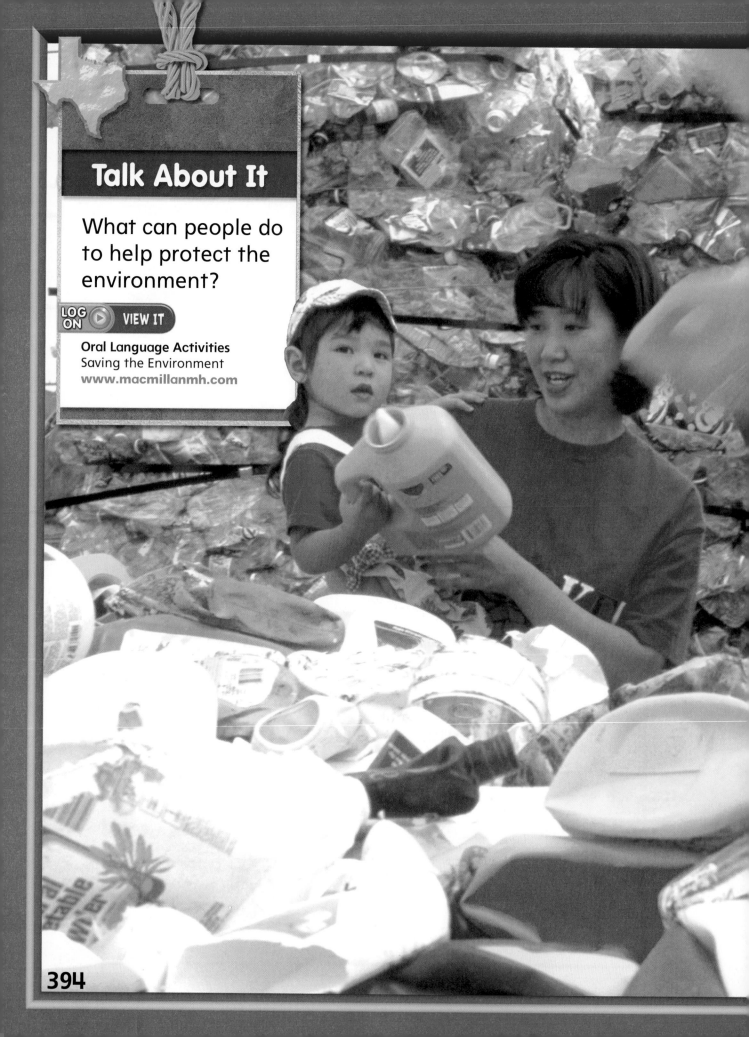

Talk About It

What can people do to help protect the environment?

LOG ON ▶ **VIEW IT**

Oral Language Activities
Saving the Environment
www.macmillanmh.com

Saving the World Around Us

Prairie Dog

Vocabulary

conservation
remains
trouble
extinct
hardest

Prairie Problem

"We really do not have a lot of time left to save the prairie," says Ron Cole. A prairie is a large, flat area covered with grasses.

Prairies have very few trees. Prairies once stretched across the middle part of the United States. Today most of that land is covered with farms and towns instead of grasses. Ron Cole belongs to a **conservation** group that teaches people to take better care of the prairie. Their goal is to protect the prairie land that **remains**. That will help the plants and animals that live there.

Ron Cole

A South Dakota prairie

396

BE CAREFUL!
WE'RE ALMOST GONE

California Condor, an endangered species

Experts warn us that many animals on our planet are in **trouble**. More than one thousand animal species are endangered! That means that they may disappear forever and become **extinct**.

It is natural for some plants and animals to become extinct. But now humans are causing more living things to become extinct than ever before. As people cut down forests, mow down prairies, or move into deserts, plants and wild animals get pushed out.

Protecting endangered species is one of the **hardest** jobs people face. The good news is that people are working to solve this problem before it gets worse.

Endangered Animals

Amphibians: about 30 species

Insects: about 50 species

Fish: about 130 species

Birds: about 275 species

Mammals: about 350 species

This chart shows the number of animal species that are endangered.

A Way to Help Planet Earth

Genre
Expository text gives information about real people, things, or events.

Text Structure
TEKS **Problem and Solution**
A problem is something that needs to be worked out. A solution is the steps taken to solve a problem.

Plastic bottles are piled high at recycling centers.

What can everyone do to help keep Earth clean?

Keeping Earth healthy is an important job. That's what environmental **conservation** is all about. People who do that job are working to keep the air, land, and water clean. They are also working to keep endangered plants and animals from becoming **extinct**.

One of the **hardest** jobs is solving the problem of trash. The **trouble** with trash is that it keeps piling up. We could run out of places to put it.

A lot of our trash comes from plastic. Soda, juice, water, shampoo—these all come in plastic bottles. Too much plastic is one of our worst trash problems. When a plastic bottle becomes trash, it **remains** trash for hundreds of years. That's because plastic doesn't change much as it gets old.

Is there a better way to deal with plastic? Yes! We can recycle it.

When we recycle, we take something that's been used and turn it into something new. An old plastic bottle can stay old and become trash. Or that old plastic bottle can be recycled and become something new.

People recycle plastic and glass at home and at school.

399

1 Plastic bottles are separated from other trash.

2 Sanitation trucks collect the recyclables.

3 Plastics are taken to a recycling center.

4 Bottles are crushed into small pieces.

Here's how it works. People save their plastic bottles. A special recycling truck picks the bottles up and takes them to the recycling center. Here the bottles are crushed into small pieces. Then the small pieces of plastic are melted down. The melted plastic is sent to a factory.

At the factory, the old plastic is made into something new. It may become a new bottle or maybe a new rug. It may become a backpack or even a slide at a playground!

5 A factory turns recycled plastic into something new and useful.

A teacher and students visit a recycling center.

Sometimes there's not much kids can do to help solve our planet's problems. But kids can do a lot about trash. Recycling is one way all people, young and old, can make a big difference!

TEKS Think and Compare

1. Where are plastics melted down?

2. What happens when something is recycled?

3. How does recycling help solve a problem with our environment?

4. Prairies are smaller, some animals are endangered, and too much plastic is being thrown away. How have humans caused these problems?

401

Answering Questions
Sometimes the answer is on the page. Sometimes it is not. You must look for clues.

These boys in Guatemala are enjoying clean water from a tap for the first time.

WATER TROUBLES

❶ Cormelia Gogu lives in Romania. Last year her school did not have clean water to drink because the water pipes were old and rusty. Workers from several countries replaced the pipes so Cormelia's school now has clean water.

❷ Cormelia does not take water for granted. But many people do. In the United States, we can just turn on a faucet to get clean water. It is not that easy in other countries.

❸ Most of Earth is covered with water, but only a small amount is safe to drink. In many places, the water is too dirty to be safe to drink. Other places receive little rainfall, so there is not enough water to grow crops.

❹ Groups such as the United Nations are working to solve these problems. People need to save water so that everyone has enough water to drink.

DIRECTIONS
Decide which is the best answer to each question.

1 Look at the chart of information from the article.

| People need clean water to drink | Dirty water is not safe to drink |

Which information belongs in the empty box?

(A) To explain how to fix rusty pipes

(B) To teach readers how to help save water

(C) To tell a story about too much rain

(D) To explain why clean water is important

2 **What is paragraph 3 mostly about?**

(A) How much water there is on Earth

(B) Crops that grow without water

(C) Why some water is not safe to drink

(D) Where dirty water comes from

3 **Why doesn't Cormelia take water for granted?**

(A) Her school has new, clean pipes.

(B) The United Nations will help her.

(C) She had dirty water at school.

(D) Her country uses rain to grow crops.

Write to a Prompt

Tom wrote about how he would take care of Earth's resources.

I stated my main idea at the beginning of my essay. I used details to support it.

We All Need the Earth

Earth has many resources. We have land, water, and air. We need to take care of these parts of Earth. We need to keep them clean.

Farmers use land to grow crops. If we put poison in the ground, crops will not grow. If we put buildings on all the land, there will be no farms. We need to save land.

We all need water. We drink it and use it to stay clean. But people waste water. If we run out of water, we cannot live.

We have to take care of the air, too. We need clean air to breathe. If we stop driving cars so much, the air will be cleaner.

We all need to save Earth's resources.

Writing Prompt

Respond in writing to the prompt below. Review the hints below before and after you write.

> Write about what people can do to keep our environment clean.

Writing Hints

- ☑ Remember to write about what people can do to keep our environment clean.
- ☑ Plan your writing by organizing your ideas.
- ☑ Include important details to support your main idea.
- ☑ Check that each sentence you write helps the reader to understand your writing.
- ☑ Use correct spelling, capitalization, punctuation, grammar, and sentences.
- ☑ Review and edit your writing.

Talk About It

What happens when a powerful storm strikes? How does this change the environment?

Oral Language Activities
Wild Weather
www.macmillanmh.com

Wild Weather

Vocabulary

violent
beware
prevent
uprooted
destroy
grasslands

TEKS **Word Parts**

A **compound word** is a word that is made up of two smaller words.

grass + lands = grasslands

Wild
Weather
Hits Florida

by Lisa O'Neil

Hurricane Charley hit Florida in 2004. It was a **violent** storm that caused a lot of damage.

News reports told people in Florida to **beware** of the storm. People had to watch out for heavy rains and strong winds. Some people tried to make sure that their homes were safe. They covered their windows with wooden boards. The boards **prevent** windows from breaking.

Heavy rains dumped water everywhere and caused floods. Powerful winds **uprooted** trees.

The trees were blown over and the roots came out of the ground. Strong winds were even able to **destroy** houses. Some were completely flattened. Hurricane Charley also damaged crops. Luckily it did not hurt any of the cows in the **grasslands**. Farmers took the animals off the grassy fields in time.

Reread for **Comprehension**

Cause → Effect

Visualize

Cause and Effect Visualizing, or forming pictures in your mind, is one way to **clarify** information in a text. Visualizing can help you identify cause and effect relationships in a text. A cause is why something happens. An effect is what happens. Use the chart to identify the causes and effects of a hurricane.

LOG ON ▶ LEARN IT Comprehension
www.macmillanmh.com

409

Comprehension

Genre
Expository text gives information and facts about a topic.

Visualize

TEKS **Cause and Effect**
As you read the selection, use the Cause and Effect Chart.

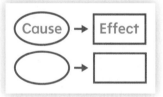

Read to Find Out
What is it like when there is a super storm?

SUPER STORMS

by Seymour Simon

Award Winning Author

The air around us is always moving and changing.
We call these changes weather.

Storms are sudden, **violent** changes in the weather.

Every second, hundreds of thunderstorms are born around the world. Thunderstorms are heavy rain showers. They can drop millions of gallons of water in just one minute.

 Cause and Effect
What is the effect of a powerful thunderstorm?

During a thunderstorm lightning bolts can shoot between clouds and the ground. A bolt of lightning is 50,000 degrees. That's five times hotter than the surface of the sun. Lightning can destroy a tree or a small house. It can also start fires in forests and grasslands.

Thunder is the sound lightning
makes as it suddenly heats the air.
You can tell how far away lightning is.
Count the seconds between the flash of
light and the sound of thunder.
Five seconds equal one mile.

Hailstones are chunks of ice that are tossed up and down by the winds of some thunderstorms.

Nearly 5,000 hailstorms strike the United States every year. They can destroy crops and damage buildings and cars.

Hail can be the size of a marble or larger than a baseball.

In July 1995, a fast-moving
group of thunderstorms hit
New York State. Winds reached
speeds of 100 miles per hour.
Over 3,000 lightning bolts
struck in one minute.
And millions of trees were
uprooted or snapped in two.

Thunderstorms sometimes give birth to tornadoes. Inside a storm, a funnel-shaped cloud reaches downward. Winds inside a tornado can spin faster than 300 miles per hour. These winds can lift cars off the ground and rip houses apart.

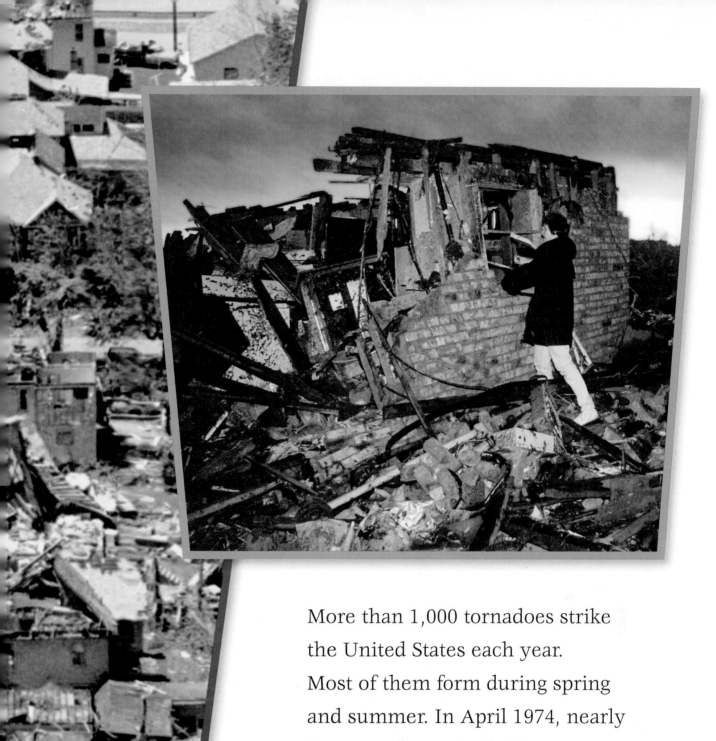

More than 1,000 tornadoes strike the United States each year. Most of them form during spring and summer. In April 1974, nearly 150 tornadoes struck 13 states east of the Mississippi River. More than 300 people were killed and 5,000 were injured. Nearly 10,000 homes were destroyed.

Television and radio stations often give early alerts. A tornado watch means that one may strike during the next few hours.

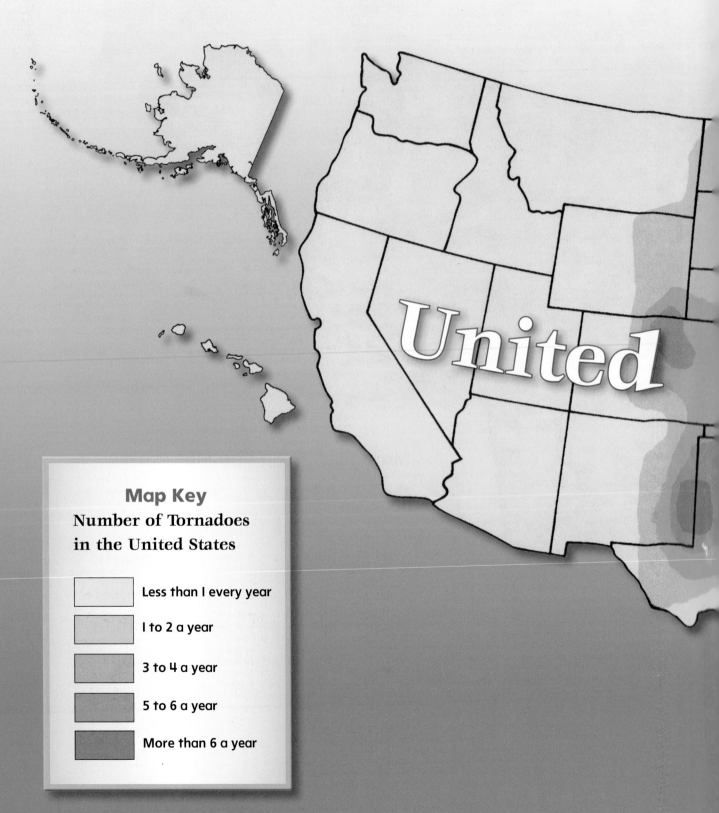

Map Key
Number of Tornadoes in the United States

Less than 1 every year

1 to 2 a year

3 to 4 a year

5 to 6 a year

More than 6 a year

A warning means a tornado has been seen by people or on radar. During a tornado warning you should find shelter in a basement or closet.

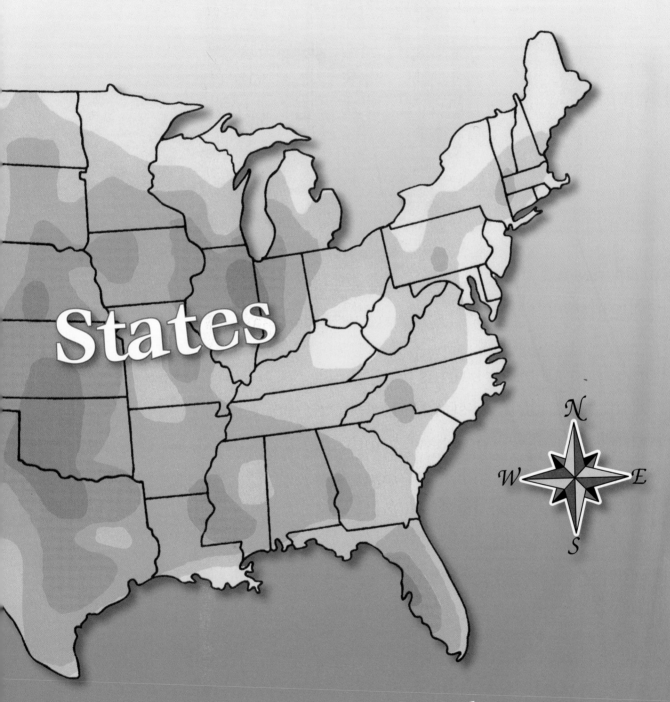

States

The map shows the number of tornadoes that hit the United States every year.

This photograph of a hurricane was taken in space looking at Earth.

Hurricanes are the deadliest storms in the world. They kill more people than all other storms combined. Hurricanes stretch for hundreds of miles. They have winds of between 74 and 200 miles per hour. The eye of a hurricane is the quiet center of the storm. Inside the eye, the wind stops blowing, the sun shines, and the sky is blue. But **beware**, the storm is not over yet.

 Cause and Effect
What kind of damage does a powerful hurricane cause?

426

Hurricanes are born over warm ocean waters from early summer to mid-fall. When they finally reach land, their pounding waves wash away beaches, boats, and houses.

Their howling winds bend and uproot trees and telephone poles. Their heavy rains cause floods.

In August 1992, Hurricane Andrew smashed into Florida and Louisiana. Over 200,000 people were left homeless.

In the Pacific Ocean, hurricanes are called typhoons. In April 1991, a typhoon hit the country of Bangladesh. Over a million homes were damaged or destroyed. More than 130,000 people died.

Blizzards are huge snowstorms.
They have winds of at least
35 miles per hour. Usually
at least two inches of snow
fall per hour. Temperatures
are at 20 degrees or lower.
Falling and blowing snow make
it hard to see in a blizzard.

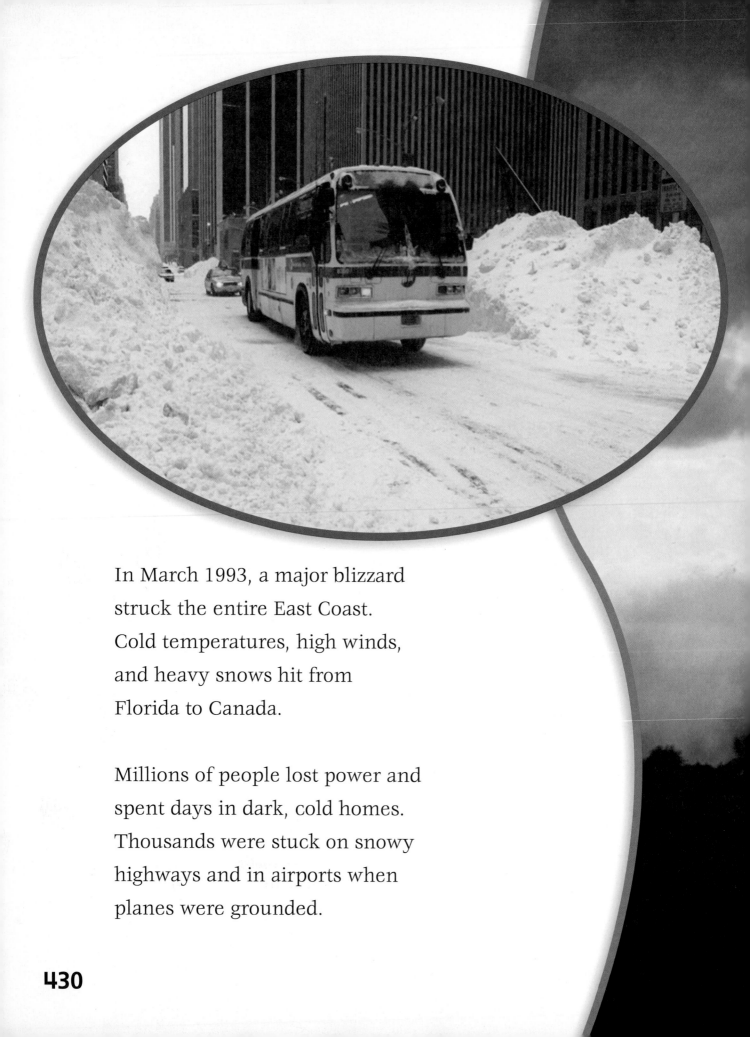

In March 1993, a major blizzard struck the entire East Coast. Cold temperatures, high winds, and heavy snows hit from Florida to Canada.

Millions of people lost power and spent days in dark, cold homes. Thousands were stuck on snowy highways and in airports when planes were grounded.

No one can prevent storms. But weather reports can predict and warn us when a storm may hit. The more prepared we are, the safer we will be when the next one strikes.

Science Facts About Seymour Simon

Seymour Simon has been writing about science for children for more than 40 years. He has written more than 200 books and is working on many more. He says that he'll never stop writing.

Seymour gets his ideas from many places. He says he was always interested in science. For example, Seymour wrote a book called *Pets in a Jar* because he collected little animals in jars as a boy. Other ideas come from his years as a science teacher. Now his grandchildren give him ideas. One grandson asked for a book about trains. *Seymour Simon's Book of Trains* was published soon after.

LOG ON ▶ FIND OUT

Author Seymour Simon
www.macmillanmh.com

Other books written by Seymour Simon

Gorillas
SEYMOUR SIMON

DESTINATION: MARS
SEYMOUR SIMON

TEKS Author's Purpose

Seymour Simon writes about storms. Think about a big storm that you watched. Write a paragraph that describes this storm.

TEKS Comprehension Check

Retell the Selection

Use the Retelling Cards to retell the selection.

Retelling Cards

Think and Compare

1. When did fast-moving thunderstorms hit New York? **Details**

2. What happens at the beginning of a tornado? What kind of damage does it leave behind? Use details from the selection to support your answer. **Cause and Effect**

3. Which storm is the most powerful in this selection? **Make Inferences**

4. What was the author's purpose in writing this selection? **Author's Purpose**

5. What information about hurricanes did you find in "Wild Weather Hits Florida" on pages 408–409 that was not in *Super Storms*? **Reading/Writing Across Texts**

Genre
Poems can describe a place by using strong words.

Literary Elements
TEKS Repetition is when a word or phrase appears two or more times in a poem.

Rhyme, rhythm, and repetition help create images in poetry.

Word Choice is important in a poem. Poets choose words carefully to give poems a certain feeling or mood.

It Fell in the City

by Eve Merriam

It fell in the city,
It fell through the night,
And the black rooftops
All turned white.

Red fire hydrants
All turned white.
Blue police cars
All turned white.

Green garbage cans
All turned white.
Gray sidewalks
All turned white.

Yellow NO PARKING signs
All turned white.
When it fell in the city
All through the night.

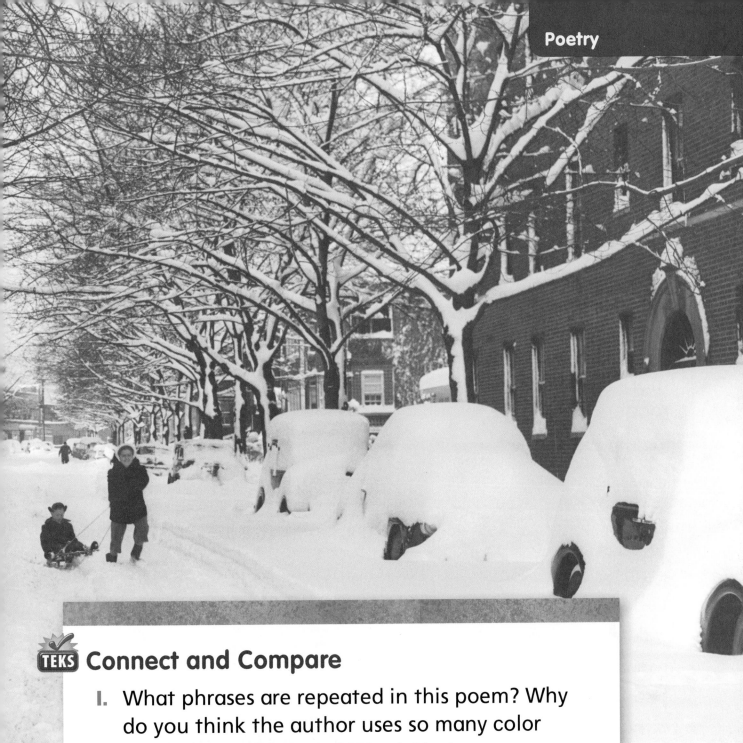

Connect and Compare

1. What phrases are repeated in this poem? Why do you think the author uses so many color words? **Repetition and Word Choice**

2. Think about this poem and *Super Storms*. Which kind of storm is described in this poem? Use details to explain how you know. **Reading/Writing Across Texts**

LOG ON ▶ FIND OUT **Poetry** Weather
www.macmillanmh.com

TEKS **Vary Sentences**

Good writers vary their sentence lengths and types so their writing will be more interesting for readers.

I begin my writing with a statement.

I include a question to vary the types of sentences in my writing.

Rain and Snow

by Pedro V.

Rain and snow are kinds of weather. Both give living things the water they need. Did you know that both rain and snow form because of the water cycle? When clouds have too much water, the water falls to Earth as rain or snow. The big difference between snow and rain is temperature. It must be below freezing for snow to fall. If it is warmer than freezing, it rains.

Your Writing Prompt

Everyone has had experiences with weather.

Think about what you know about different kinds of weather.

Write a paragraph that compares two kinds of weather.

Writer's Checklist

☑ My writing is a paragraph that clearly compares two kinds of weather.

☑ I **vary the sentence** lengths and types to make my writing interesting.

☑ I include details that support the main idea of my paragraph.

☑ I use capital letters and punctuation marks in the right places. I use adjectives that compare correctly.

EXPLAINING NATURE

Talk About It

Describe what you can see in the sky. How did the people of long ago explain the natural world?

LOG ON ▶ **VIEW IT**

Oral Language Activities
Explaining Nature
www.macmillanmh.com

WHY SUN AND MOON LIVE IN THE SKY

Characters

Narrator   Moon

Sun   Water

Scene One: Sun and Moon's house

Narrator: Long ago Sun and Moon lived on Earth.

Moon: Sun, I see a **signal** in the sky. It is a sign.

Sun: Yes, clouds do not take those shapes **randomly**. The clouds do not look that way by accident. Water controls the clouds. I think he is asking me to visit.

Narrator: Sun and Water were friends. But Water never visited Sun and Moon's house.

Scene Two: The next day at Water's house

Sun: Water, please come visit our house.

Water: Your house is too small. I don't fit inside.

Sun: Moon and I will build a big new house so you can visit.

Scene Three: Sun and Moon's house

Narrator: Later, Sun told Moon his plan. Moon thought it was a good idea so she **agreed** to help. They decided to build the house with trees.

Moon: I **gathered** the wood and put it all together.

Sun: Please help me carry it. The ends keep **jabbing** and poking me.

Scene Four: Later at Sun and Moon's new house

Narrator: At last, Sun and Moon finished their new house. It was time for Water to visit.

Water: Hello, friends. May I come in?

Narrator: Water entered the house and filled every corner. The house was still too small. There was no room left for Sun and Moon. So, they flew to the sky, where they still are today.

Reread for **Comprehension**

Visualize

Problem and Solution Forming pictures in your mind can help you visualize the events in a story. A character in a story usually has a problem and must take steps to solve it. Reread the play and use the chart to help identify the problem and the steps taken to reach a solution.

Problem
↓
Steps to Solution
↓
Solution

LOG ON ► LEARN IT Comprehension
www.macmillanmh.com

Comprehension

Genre
A **Play** is a story that can be acted out.

Visualize
TEKS **Problem and Solution**
As you read, use your Problem and Solution Chart.

Problem
↓
Steps to Solution
↓
Solution

Read to Find Out
What is the characters' problem? How do they solve it?

Pushing Up the Sky

BY JOSEPH BRUCHAC

ILLUSTRATED BY STEFANO VITALE

Award Winning Author

SNOHOMISH

The Snohomish people lived in the area of the Northwest that is now known as the state of Washington. They fished in the ocean and **gathered** food from the shore. Their homes and many of the things they used every day, such as bowls and canoe paddles, were carved from the trees.

Like many of the other peoples of the area, they also carved totem poles, which recorded the history and stories of their nation. *Pushing Up the Sky* is a Snohomish story carved into a totem pole in Everett, Washington.

Speaking Roles: Narrator, Tall Man, Girl, Mother, Boy, First Chief, Second Chief, Third Chief, Fourth Chief, Fifth Chief, Sixth Chief, and Seventh Chief

Non-Speaking Roles: Animals and Birds. They include dog, deer, elk, goat, lion, rabbit, hawk, eagle, and seagull.

Scenery: The village can be a painted backdrop showing houses among trees. The ocean is in the background.

Costumes: People can wear blankets or towels. Chiefs wear them around their shoulders, and other humans wear them around their waists. The animal characters can wear face paint or masks made from paper plates.

TEKS Locate Facts
Locating facts helps us understand the story. Look at page 444. What fact can you find about where the Snohomish people live?

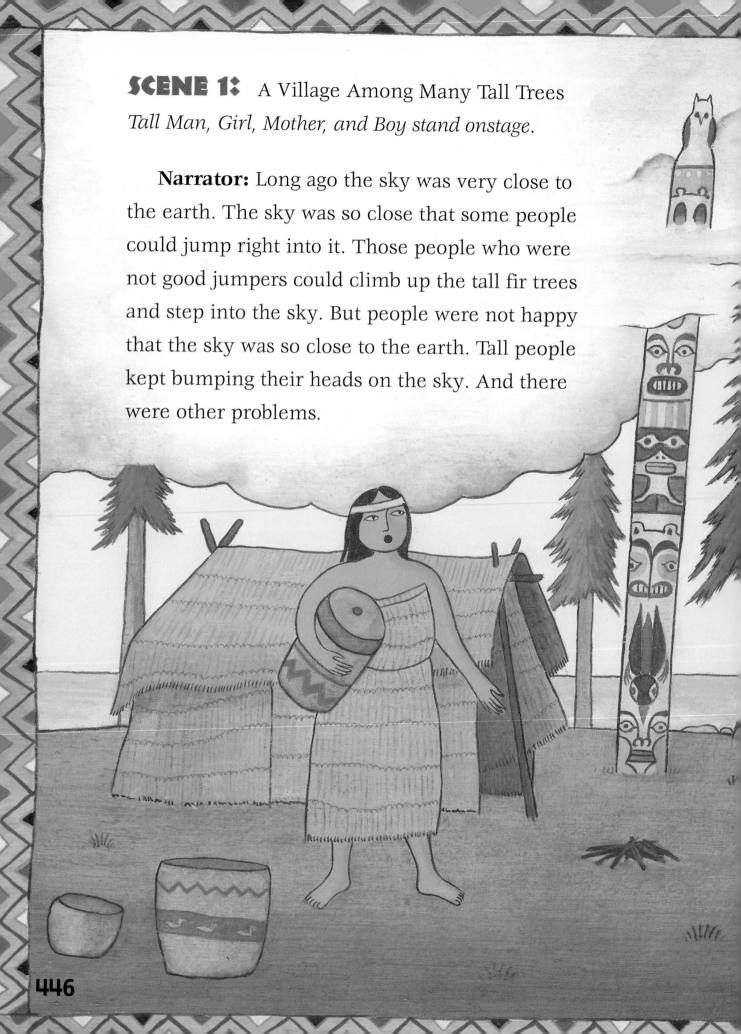

SCENE 1: A Village Among Many Tall Trees

Tall Man, Girl, Mother, and Boy stand onstage.

Narrator: Long ago the sky was very close to the earth. The sky was so close that some people could jump right into it. Those people who were not good jumpers could climb up the tall fir trees and step into the sky. But people were not happy that the sky was so close to the earth. Tall people kept bumping their heads on the sky. And there were other problems.

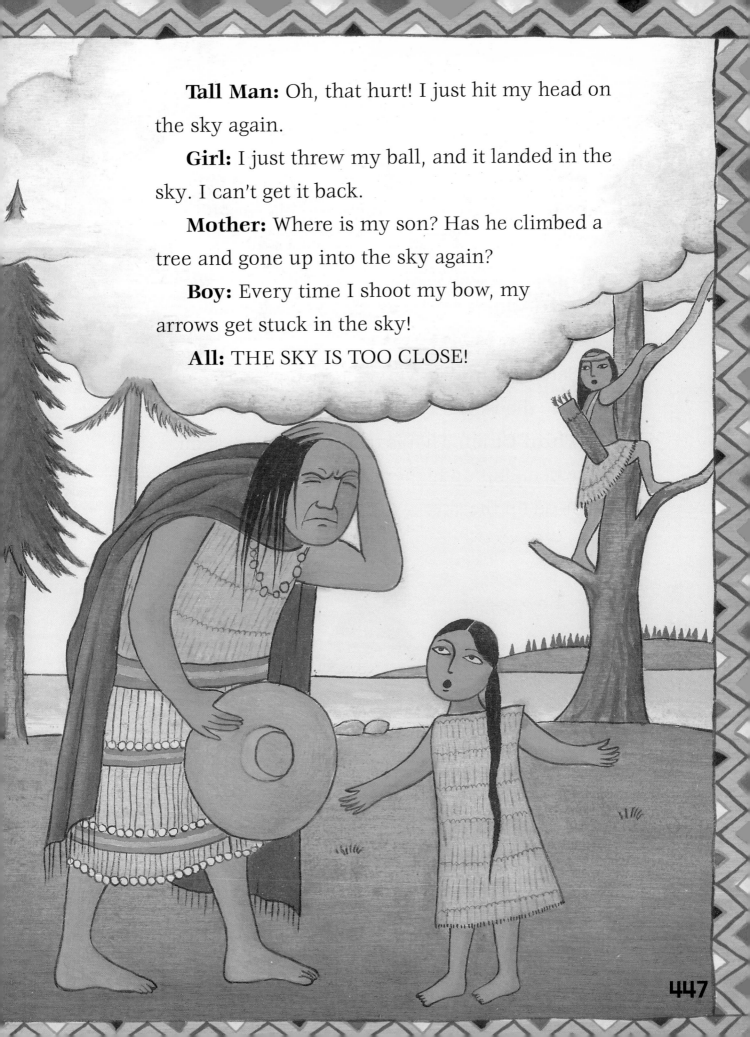

Tall Man: Oh, that hurt! I just hit my head on the sky again.

Girl: I just threw my ball, and it landed in the sky. I can't get it back.

Mother: Where is my son? Has he climbed a tree and gone up into the sky again?

Boy: Every time I shoot my bow, my arrows get stuck in the sky!

All: THE SKY IS TOO CLOSE!

447

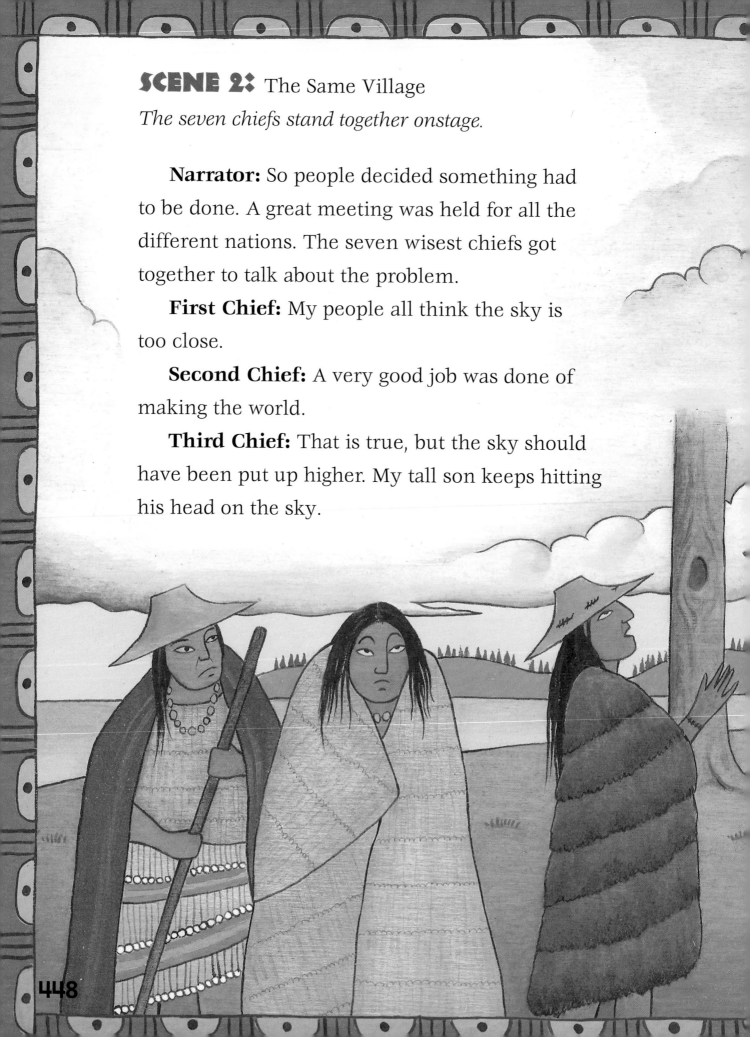

SCENE 2: The Same Village

The seven chiefs stand together onstage.

Narrator: So people decided something had to be done. A great meeting was held for all the different nations. The seven wisest chiefs got together to talk about the problem.

First Chief: My people all think the sky is too close.

Second Chief: A very good job was done of making the world.

Third Chief: That is true, but the sky should have been put up higher. My tall son keeps hitting his head on the sky.

Fourth Chief: My daughter keeps losing her ball in the sky.

Fifth Chief: People keep going up into the sky when they should be staying on the earth to help each other.

Sixth Chief: When mothers look for their children, they cannot find them because they are up playing in the sky.

Seventh Chief: We are **agreed**, then. The sky is too close.

All: WE ARE AGREED.

TEKS Problem and Solution
Describe the problem that the characters must solve.

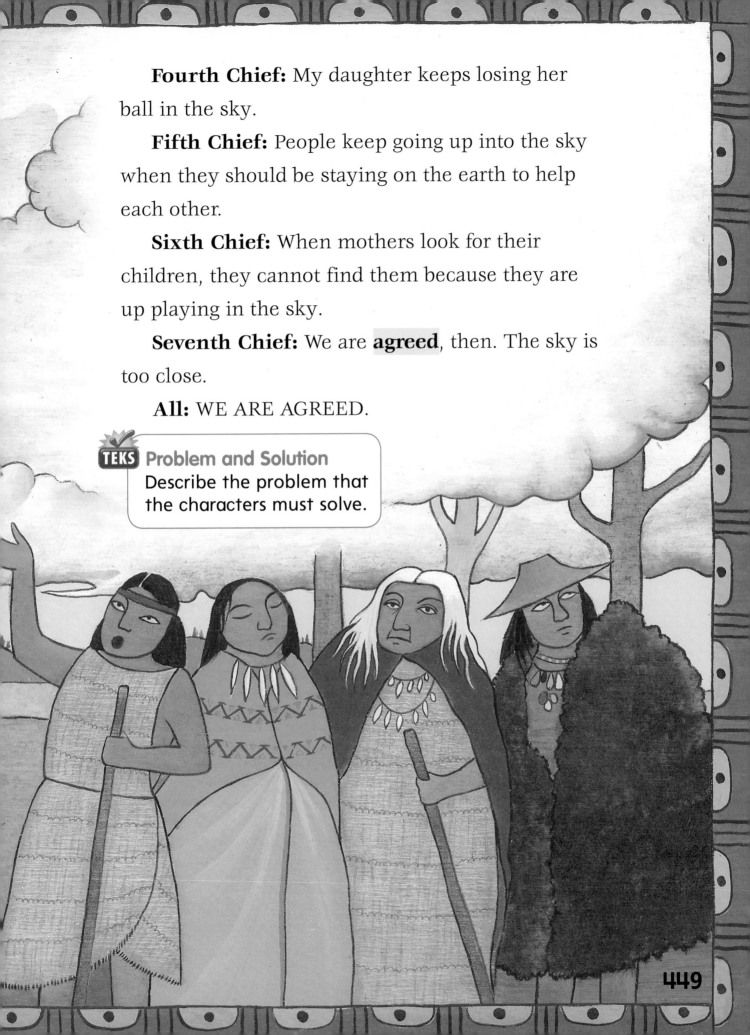

449

Second Chief: What can we do?

Seventh Chief: I have an idea. Let's push up the sky.

Third Chief: The sky is heavy.

Seventh Chief: If we all push together, we can do it.

Sixth Chief: We will ask the birds and animals to help. They also do not like it that the sky is so close.

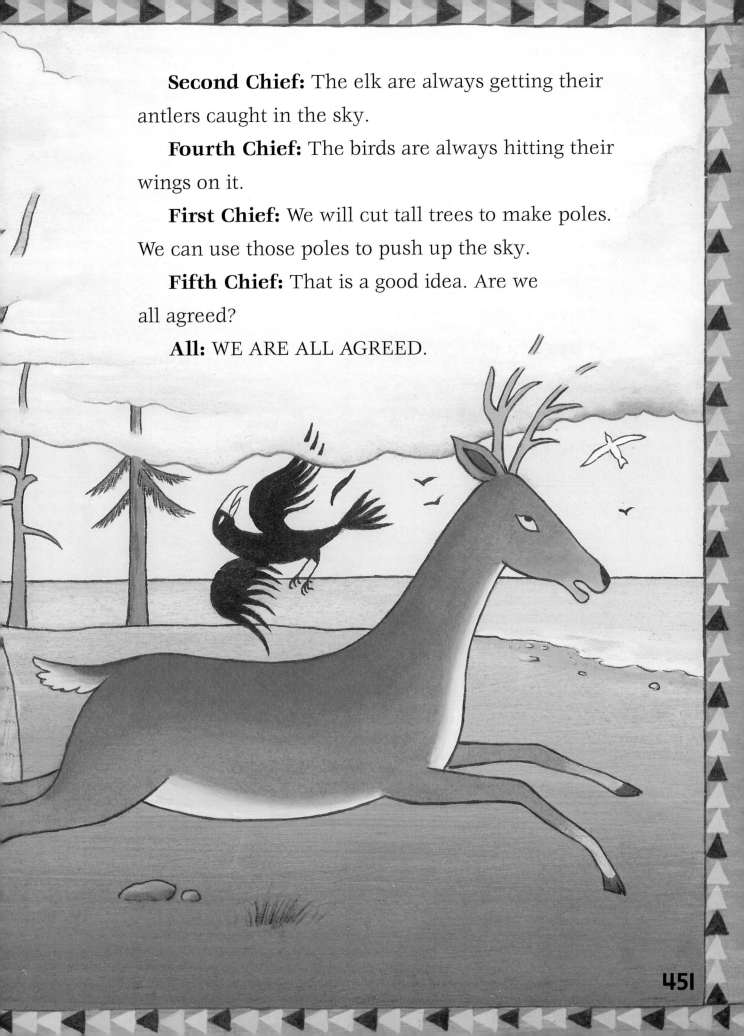

Second Chief: The elk are always getting their antlers caught in the sky.

Fourth Chief: The birds are always hitting their wings on it.

First Chief: We will cut tall trees to make poles. We can use those poles to push up the sky.

Fifth Chief: That is a good idea. Are we all agreed?

All: WE ARE ALL AGREED.

SCENE 3: The Same Village

All the people, except Seventh Chief, are gathered together. They hold long poles. The Birds and Animals are with them. They all begin pushing **randomly***. They are* **jabbing** *their poles into the air. (The sky can be imagined as just above them.)*

Girl: It isn't working!

Boy: The sky is still too close.

Fifth Chief: Where is Seventh Chief? This was his idea!

Seventh Chief (entering): Here I am. I had to find this long pole.

TEKS Problem and Solution

Identify the steps the characters take to solve their problem.

452

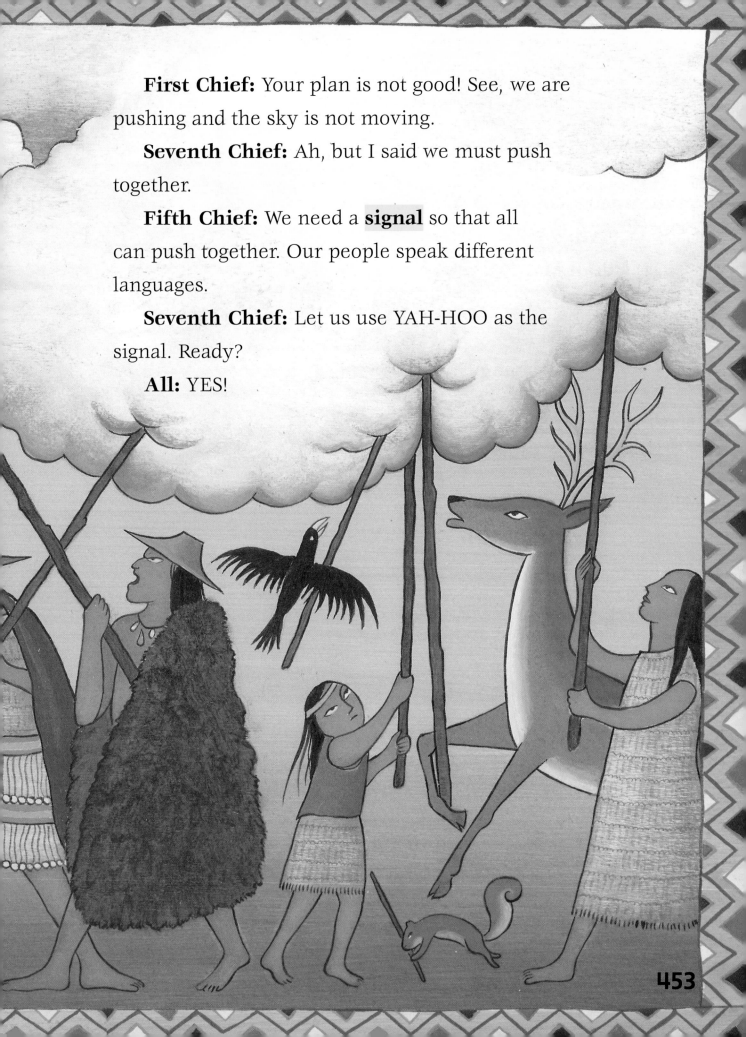

First Chief: Your plan is not good! See, we are pushing and the sky is not moving.

Seventh Chief: Ah, but I said we must push together.

Fifth Chief: We need a **signal** so that all can push together. Our people speak different languages.

Seventh Chief: Let us use YAH-HOO as the signal. Ready?

All: YES!

453

Seventh Chief: YAH-HOO.

At the signal everyone pushes together.

All: YAH-HOO!

Seventh Chief: YAH-HOO.

Again everyone pushes together.

All: YAH-HOO!

Tall Man: We are doing it!

Mother: Now my son won't be able to hide in the sky!

Seventh Chief: YAH-HOO.

Again everyone pushes together.

All: YAH-HOO!

Boy: It will be too high for my arrows to stick into it.

Seventh Chief: YAH-HOO.

Again everyone pushes together.

All: YAH-HOOOO!

First Chief: We have done it!

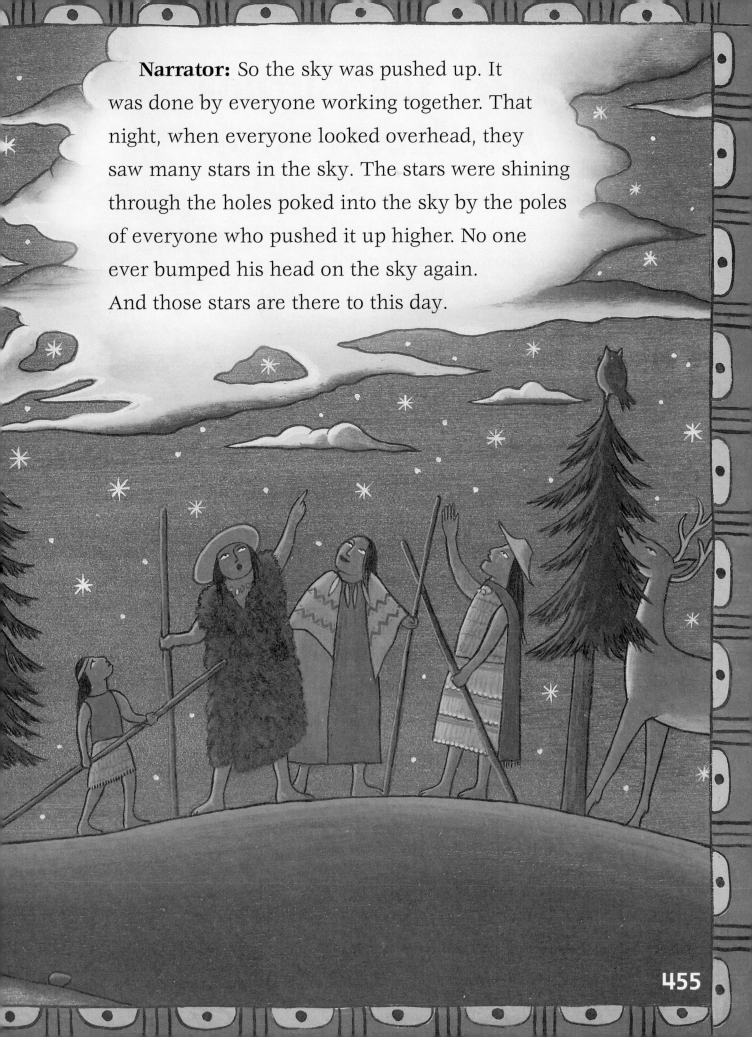

Narrator: So the sky was pushed up. It was done by everyone working together. That night, when everyone looked overhead, they saw many stars in the sky. The stars were shining through the holes poked into the sky by the poles of everyone who pushed it up higher. No one ever bumped his head on the sky again. And those stars are there to this day.

Meet the Author and Illustrator

Joseph Bruchac writes stories, plays, poems, and articles for children and adults. He is also a storyteller and performs around the country. Joseph is an Abenaki Native American. All of his work centers on keeping alive the Abenaki culture and that of other Native American peoples.

Stefano Vitale grew up in Italy, where he studied art. Stefano especially likes to create pictures on wood. "There is an ancient quality to wood. It has wisdom and age," he says.

Other books written by Joseph Bruchac

LOG ON ▶ FIND OUT

Author Joseph Bruchac
Illustrator Stefano Vitale
www.macmillanmh.com

Author's Purpose
Joseph Bruchac tells a story about people working together. Think about a sport or an activity that you do with others. Write a paragraph about how you work together.

TEKS Comprehension Check

Retell the Story

Use the Retelling Cards to retell the story.

Retelling Cards

Think and Compare

1. Who did the Sixth Chief want to call on for help? **Details**

2. What is the main problem in this story? What steps do the characters take to solve it? Use details to support your answers. **Problem and Solution**

Problem
↓
Steps to Solution
↓
Solution

3. Why is it important for the people to have a **signal** to push up the sky? **Make Inferences**

4. Without the Seventh Chief, the first plan did not work. What does the the author want readers to learn? **Author's Purpose**

5. Joseph Bruchac also wrote "The Storytelling Stone." How are the settings of *Pushing Up the Sky* and that story the same? How are they different? In what ways are the plots similar? In what ways are they different? **Reading/Writing Across Texts**

GETTING TO KNOW JOSEPH BRUCHAC

BY CHRIS LOBACK

Joseph Bruchac is the **author** who wrote *Pushing Up the Sky*. To learn more about Mr. Bruchac, we **interviewed** him. We asked him questions about his work, and he answered them. In this interview the words after **Q:** are the questions the interviewer asked. The words after **A:** are Joseph Bruchac's answer.

Q: Why do you write Native American stories?

A: I think that they **appeal** to a lot of people. Children and adults have told me that they like to read them. Native American stories are fun to hear and also teach good lessons.

Q: Why do you write plays?

A: I write plays for two reasons. The first is that many teachers told me it was hard to find good Native American plays for kids. The second reason is that I love to give kids the chance to take part in a story.

Q: Which of your stories do you like the best?

A: My favorites are the stories with monsters and scary events in them. One of these is *Skeleton Man*. I like this scary story because it shows how even a child can beat a monster if she does the right thing!

 Connect and Compare

1. What is one reason Joseph Bruchac writes plays? **Interview**

2. Think about this interview and *Pushing Up the Sky*. Explain why this may be one of Joseph Bruchac's favorite stories. **Reading/Writing Across Texts**

 Social Studies Activities

With a partner, find and read another play by Joseph Bruchac.

LOG ON ▶ FIND OUT **Social Studies** Plays
www.macmillanmh.com

TEKS Sequence of Events

Good writers make the **sequence of events** in a play clear by telling them in the correct order.

Reading and Writing Connection

The beginning tells what the characters say first.

My ending describes the last event in the play.

Sun and Wind
by Joe M.

Characters: Narrator, Wind, Sun, Man

Narrator: Wind and Sun are fighting loudly.

Wind: I am stronger than you, Sun.

Sun: No, you're not, Wind. Prove it.

Wind: Do you see that man? Whoever can make him take off his coat is stronger. I'll go first.

Man: Brrrr. The wind is cold. I will button up my coat to keep warm.

Wind: I give up. It's your turn, Sun.

Man: The sun is out. Now it is warm. I will take off this heavy coat.

Wind: You win, Sun. You are stronger.

Your Writing Prompt

A play includes at least one character who speaks.

Think about characters that you might like to write about.

Write a play with characters who speak to one another.

Writer's Checklist

☑ My play includes characters who speak to one another.

☑ My play includes a clear sequence of events.

☑ I include details, such as each character's name, before he or she speaks.

☑ I use the correct punctuation, including a colon after each character's name, when he or she speaks. My adverbs are correct.

TEKS

Review

Author's Purpose
Problem and Solution
Compare and Contrast
Chart
Compound Words

Rico's ZEBRA

"Today we're going to use our art materials to make the animals we read about today," Mrs. Baxter told her students. "I want each of you to pick an animal you like," Mrs. Baxter said. "You can use any art materials you want."

There were many good artists in Rico's class, but Rico didn't think he was one of them. "I'll watch how the good artists make animals. Maybe that will help me draw a zebra."

Rico watched Jen drawing an elephant with a marker. Her lines were dark and strong. Her elephant looked great. Rico tried drawing a zebra the same way. But his lines came out too thick and wavy.

In 1965, Ann and her mother started selling handmade carriers. When the baby carrier appeared in a catalog, many people wanted it.

Ann received a patent for the baby carrier in 1969. By that time the baby carrier had leg holes and straps that could be made longer or shorter. It could also be worn on the back or front.

Ann Moore's baby carriers were very useful to parents.

By 1979, the baby carriers were made in a factory. More than 25,000 were sold every month. In 1985, Ann sold the company.

Now, all over the world, babies ride in baby carriers, safe and happy, close to their parents.

YEAR	EVENT
early 1960s	Ann Moore is a nurse in Africa.
1964	Ann has a baby.
1965	Ann sells handmade baby carriers.
1969	Ann patents her baby carrier.
1979	Baby carriers are made in factories.
1985	Ann sells her company.

Comprehension

Compare Stories

- Good readers compare characters, settings, and plot when looking at two versions of the same story.

- With a partner, reread "Chicken Little" and "Foolish, Timid Rabbit" on pages 162–165. Then discuss how these two stories are similar. Write similarities between characters, settings, and plot on a separate piece of paper. Share details with your classmates.

Writing

Write a Persuasive Essay

- Write a persuasive essay about how and why you can help the environment either at home or at school. Include reasons to support your point of view.

Word Study

Phonics

Consonants -*le*, -*el*, -*al*, and Final e Syllables

- Review the following words: *puddle*, *several*, *rattle*, *jiggle*, *apple*, *female*, *replace*, and *inside*. Say each word aloud and identify the -*le*, -*el*, -*al*, and final e syllables.

- On a separate piece of paper, write the correct word that belongs in each blank below. Have a partner check your answers.

  1. I ate the juicy, red _____.

  2. The phone rang _____ times.

  3. Stay _____ during a storm.

Spelling

Words with -*le*, -*el*, and -*al*, and Final e

- Use the spelling words listed above to write a short story about a powerful storm.

Glossary

What Is a Glossary?

A glossary can help you find the **meanings** of words. If you see a word that you don't know, try to find it in the glossary. The words are in **alphabetical order**. **Guide words** at the top of each page tell you the first and last words on the page.

A **definition** is given for each word. An **example** shows the word used in a sentence. Each word is divided into **syllables**. Finally, the **part of speech** is given.

mammal

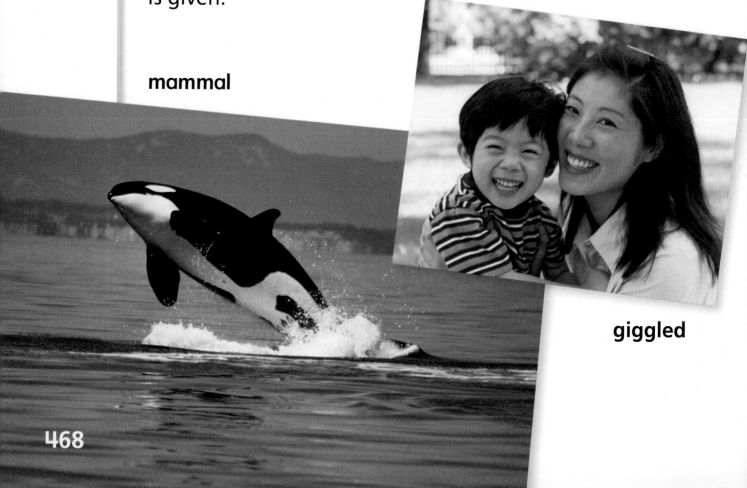

giggled

Guide Words

First word on the page   Last word on the page

Sample Entry

Definition

Main entry — **burrow**   A hole dug in the ground by an animal. *A gopher lives in an*

Example sentence — *underground* **burrow**.

Syllable division — **bur•row** *noun.* ————— Part of speech

desert

Aa

accident   A sudden event resulting in loss or injury. *I tripped by accident and broke my leg.* **ac·ci·dent** *noun.*

adapted   Made or became used to. *When he moved to Alaska, he adapted to the cold weather.* **a·dapt·ed** *verb.* Past tense of **adapt**.

agreed   Thought or felt the same way as someone else. *My friends all agreed it was a good book.* **a·greed** *verb.* Past tense of **agree**.

aid   To give help. *I aid my grandmother with some household chores.* **aid** *verb.*

ancient   Having to do with times very long ago. *Scientists found an ancient city buried under layers of dirt.* **an·cient** *adjective.*

appeal   To be attractive or interesting. *Does playing a board game appeal to you now?* **ap·peal** *verb.*

aroma   A pleasant or agreeable smell. *The flowers gave off a wonderful aroma.* **a·ro·ma** *noun.*

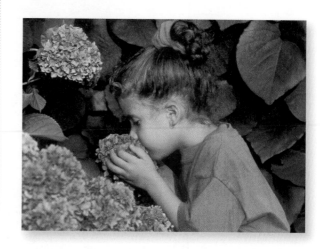

assembled   Met together for a purpose. *The crowd assembled in the auditorium for the meeting.* **as·sem·bled** *verb.* Past tense of **assemble**.

attached   Fastened. *Pedro attached his poster to the wall with tape.* **at·tached** *verb.* Past tense of **attach**.

attention The act of watching or listening carefully. *The clown held the children's* **attention** *with his balloon shapes.*
at·ten·tion *noun.*

author A person who has written a story, play, article, or poem. *Peggy Rathmann is the* **author** *of Officer Buckle and Gloria.*
au·thor *noun.*

Bb

beasts Animals that have four feet. *Many* **beasts** *live at the zoo.*
beasts *plural noun.* Plural of **beast**.

beloved Loved a lot. *The class pet was* **beloved** *by the students.*
be·lov·ed *adjective.*

beware To be on one's guard; be careful. ***Beware** of speeding cars when crossing the street.*
be·ware *verb.*

beyond Farther on. *Look* **beyond** *the desert and you'll see the mountains.*
be·yond *preposition, adverb.*

blooming Having flowers. *The rose bushes will be* **blooming** *in June.*
bloom·ing *adjective.*

buddy A close friend. *His* **buddy** *goes camping with him.*
bud·dy *noun.*

burrow A hole dug in the ground by an animal. *A gopher lives in an underground* **burrow**.
bur·row *noun.*

471

burst   To break open suddenly. *The bag **burst** because I put too much in it.*
burst *verb.*

Cc

calm   Not excited or nervous. *Because we stayed **calm** during the fire, we got out safely.*
calm *adjective.*

condensation   The conversion of water from a gas into a liquid. *I saw **condensation** on my glass.*
con·den·sa·tion *noun.*

confirm   To show to be true or correct. *Tomorrow's newspaper will **confirm** the report of a fire downtown.*
con·firm *verb.*

conservation   The wise use of the forests, rivers, minerals, and other natural resources of a country. *Water **conservation** is an important issue in many countries.*
con·ser·va·tion *noun.*

cowboys   Those who tend cattle or horses. *The **cowboys** rounded up the cattle.*
cow·boys *plural noun.* Plural of **cowboy**.

Dd

delicious   Pleasing or delightful to taste or smell. *The warm apple pie smelled **delicious**.*
de·li·cious *adjective.*

desert   A hot, dry, sandy area of land with few or no plants growing on it. *Plants that need a lot of water will not grow in a **desert**.*
des·ert *noun.*

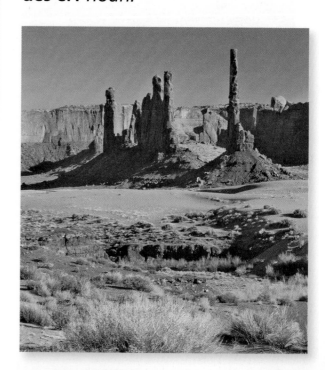

destroy   To ruin completely. *A hurricane can destroy a building.*

de·stroy *verb.*

devoured   Ate or consumed. *The hungry teenager devoured the sandwiches.*

de·voured *verb.* Past tense of **devour.**

distant   Far away in distance or time; not near. *Some of our distant relatives live in Australia.*

dis·tant *adjective.*

drifts   Moves because of a current of air or water. *When I stop rowing, my canoe drifts along the river.*

drifts *verb.* Present tense of **drift.**

drowns   To die by staying underwater and not being able to breathe. *A lifeguard watches the pool carefully to make sure that no one drowns.*

drowns *verb.* Present tense of **drown.**

Ee

enormous   Much greater than the usual size; very large. *Some dinosaurs were enormous compared with animals today.*

e·nor·mous *adjective.*

evaporate   The change from a liquid state to a vapor state. *The water began to evaporate from the puddles in the street.*

evap·o·rate *verb.*

examines   Looks at closely and carefully. *The coach always examines the hockey sticks to make sure they are not broken.* **ex·am·ines** *verb.* Present tense of **examine.**

extinct   When a thing dies out and no more of its kind are living anywhere on Earth. *Dinosaurs are extinct.* **ex·tinct** *adjective.*

Ff

fetch   To go after and bring back; get. *Please fetch two more plates from the kitchen.* **fetch** *verb.*

fluttered   Moved or flew with quick, light, flapping movements. *Moths fluttered around the light.* **flut·tered** *verb.* Past tense of **flutter.**

force   Strength or power. *Wind can have great force.* **force** *noun.*

frantically   Done in a way that is excited by worry or fear. *Maria searched frantically for her keys.* **fran·tic·al·ly** *adverb.*

friction   A rubbing that can slow things. *When I use my feet to stop my bike, I use friction.* **fric·tion** *noun.*

Gg

gas   A substance that spreads to fill a space. *Balloons are filled with air, which is a kind of gas.* **gas** *noun.*

gasped Said while breathing in suddenly or with effort. *"Help!" gasped the struggling child.*
gasped *verb.* Past tense of **gasp**.

gathered Brought together. *Carol gathered her favorite books to read on vacation.*
gath·ered *verb.* Past tense of **gather**.

gently Done carefully not to hurt someone or something. *Christopher gently stroked the kitten.*
gen·tly *adverb.*

giggled Laughed in a silly or nervous way. *I giggled at my mom's funny joke.*
gig·gled *verb.* Past tense of **giggle**.

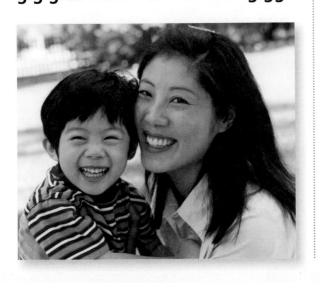

glanced Took a quick look. *The driver glanced behind her before safely changing lanes.*
glanced *verb.* Past tense of **glance**.

gleamed Glowed or shone. *The new bike gleamed in the sunlight.*
gleamed *verb.* Past tense of **gleam**.

grasslands Lands covered mainly with grass, where animals feed. *Scientists are trying to protect U.S. grasslands.*
grass·lands *plural noun.* Plural of **grassland**.

gravity The force that pulls things to Earth and keeps them from floating off into space. *Gravity keeps our feet on the ground.*
grav·ity *noun.*

475

Hh

habitats Places where plants and animals live. *Some of the animals' habitats are warm and humid while others are cold and dry.* **hab·i·tats** *plural noun.* Plural of **habitat.**

handy Within reach. *Dad keeps his car keys handy in his front pocket.* **han·dy** *adjective.*

hardest Needing or using a lot of work. *My hardest chore is cleaning out the garage.* **har·dest** *adjective.* Superlative of **hard.**

hatches Comes from an egg. *The baby bird hatches from its egg when it is ready.* **hatches** *verb.* Present tense of **hatch.**

hazards Things that can cause harm or injury. *Ice, snow, rain, and fog are hazards to drivers.* **haz·ards** *plural noun.* Plural of **hazard.**

heal To become well or healthy again. *My cut will heal after I put a bandage on it.* **heal** *verb.*

hopeful Wanting or believing that something wished for will happen. *We are hopeful that the rain will stop before the field hockey game starts.* **hope·ful** *adjective.*

hunger Pain or weakness caused by not eating enough food. *Some wild animals die from hunger.* **hun·ger** *noun.*

Ii

informs   Gives information to. *The firefighter **informs** the class about fire safety.*

in·forms *verb.* Present tense of **inform**.

interviewed   Asked questions to get information. *I **interviewed** the principal for the school newspaper.*

in·ter·viewed *verb.* Past tense of **interview**.

itches   Tickling or stinging feelings in the skin. *Kim rubbed her back to scratch her **itches**.*

itch·es *plural noun.* Plural of **itch**.

Jj

jabbing   Poking with something pointed. *Jason moved his books so they weren't **jabbing** into his side.*

jab·bing *verb.* Inflected form of **jab**.

Ll

lengthy   Being very long in distance or time. *The kangaroo made **lengthy** leaps to cross the field quickly.*

length·y *adjective.*

liquids   Materials that are wet and flow. *Water and juice are examples of **liquids**.*

liq·uids *plural noun.* Plural of **liquid**.

Mm

mammal   A kind of animal that is warm-blooded and has a backbone. Female mammals make milk to feed their young. Most mammals are covered with fur or have some hair. *My teacher told me that a whale is a **mammal**, but a fish is not.*
mam·mal *noun.*

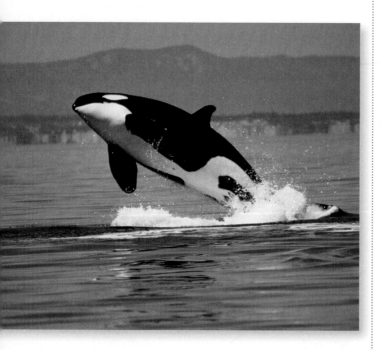

menu   A list of food offered in a restaurant. *Patricia likes to read the whole **menu** before choosing what to eat.*
men·u *noun.*

minerals   Something found in nature that is not an animal or a plant. *Salt, coal, and gold are **minerals**.*
min·er·als *plural noun.* Plural of **mineral**.

muscles   Bundles of tissue that move certain parts of the body. *My aunt goes to the gym every day to keep her **muscles** strong.*
mu·scles *plural noun.* Plural of **muscle**.

Nn

neighbor   A person, place, or thing that is near another. *A new **neighbor** moved in next door.*
neigh·bor *noun.*

nibble   To eat quickly and with small bites. *A mouse will **nibble** cheese.*
nib·ble *verb.*

noble   Impressive looking. *The **noble** lion stood proudly at the opening to the cave.*
no·ble *adjective.*

nocturnal
Being seen or happening at night. *Owls are **nocturnal** animals.*
noc·tur·nal *adjective.*

normal   Having or showing average health and growth. *The doctor said that it is **normal** for a baby to cry.*
nor·mal *adjective.*

Oo

obeys   Does what one is told to do. *The dog **obeys** me when I tell him to stop running.*
o·beys *verb.* Present tense of **obey**.

Pp

patterns   The way colors, shapes, and lines are placed. *I like **patterns** with dots and stripes.*
pat·terns *plural noun.* Plural of **pattern**.

peered   Looked at closely to see clearly. *Carlos **peered** through a telescope to study the stars.*
peered *verb.* Past tense of **peer**.

personal   Having to do with a person. *Denise kept her voice low so no one could hear her **personal** information when she talked on the phone.*
per·son·al *adjective.*

plant To put or set in the ground. *I wanted to* ***plant*** *the daffodils in my garden.*
plant *noun.*

preen To make oneself smooth or sleek. *Birds* ***preen*** *by washing and smoothing their feathers.*
preen *verb.*

prevent To keep something from happening. *A seat belt will help* ***prevent*** *an injury in a car accident.*
prevent *verb.*

prey An animal that is hunted by another animal for food. *Rabbits, birds, and snakes are the* ***prey*** *of foxes.*
prey *noun.*

prickly Having small, sharp thorns or points. *The cactus plants are* ***prickly***.
prick·ly *adjective.*

promised Said that something will or will not happen. *I* ***promised*** *that I would clean my room.*
prom·ised *verb.* Past tense of **promise**.

puddles Small, shallow pools of water or other liquids. *Our driveway has many* **puddles** *after a storm.*

pud·dles *plural noun.* Plural of **puddle**.

Rr

randomly Made or done by chance, with no clear pattern. *The teacher* **randomly** *called three students to the front of the room.*

ran·dom·ly *adverb.*

recognized Knew and remembered from before. *I* **recognized** *my teacher standing in line at the movies.*

rec·og·nized *verb.* Past tense of **recognize**.

remains Things that are left. *The explorers found the* **remains** *of an ancient building.*

re·mains *noun.*

rescued Saved or freed. *The firefighter* **rescued** *the cat that had been stuck in the tree.*

res·cued *verb.* Past tense of **rescue**.

roam   To move from place to place without somewhere special to go. *The cows **roam** all over the fields as they eat.*

roam *verb.*

route   A road or other course used for traveling. *We took a different **route** to the beach because of the traffic.*

route *noun.*

Ss

scent   A smell. *The **scent** of roses filled the air.*

scent *noun.*

seed   The part of a plant from which a new plant will grow. *We planted a pumpkin **seed** in the garden to try to grow pumpkins next year.*

seed *noun.*

serious   Dangerous. *The doctor told us that cancer is a **serious** illness.*

se·ri·ous *adjective.*

signal   A way of showing people to do something. *A red traffic light is a **signal** to stop.*

sig·nal *noun.*

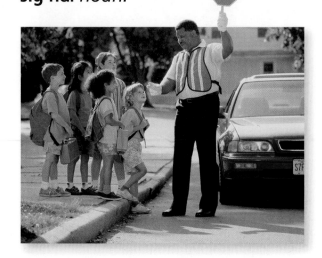

simmered   Cooked at or just below the boiling point. *The soup **simmered** on the stove all day.*

sim·mered *verb.* Past tense of **simmer.**

site   A place where something has happened or will happen. *The battle **site** is just outside the castle's wall.*

site *noun.*

snuggled   Lay close together or held closely for warmth or protection, or to show love. *I* **snuggled** *up against my mom during the thunderstorm.*

snug·gled *verb.* Past tense of **snuggle**.

solids   Firm materials with definite shape. *Rocks are examples of* **solids.**

solids *plural noun.* Plural of **solid**.

stages   The different steps or times in a process. *During all* **stages** *of growth, a flower needs water.*

stag·es *plural noun.* Plural of **stage**.

sunlight   The light of the sun. *We enjoyed the bright* **sunlight** *at the beach.*

sun·light *noun.*

swung   Moved back and forth. *We* **swung** *back and forth on the monkey bars.*

swung *verb.* Past tense of **swing**.

Tt

temperature   A measure of how hot or cold something is. *You can find the temperature by using a thermometer.*

tem·per·a·ture *noun.*

tips   Some helpful information. *My teacher gave me some tips for how to spell better.*

tips *plural noun.* Plural of **tip**.

trade   Giving one thing in return for something else. *Swapping an apple for an orange is a fair trade.*

trade *noun.*

trouble   A difficult or dangerous condition. *We'll be in trouble if we don't complete the work.*

trou·ble *noun.*

Uu

unable   Not having the power or skill to do something; not able. *I was unable to reach the light switch because it was too high.*

un·a·ble *adjective.*

uprooted   Torn or pulled up by the roots. *A bulldozer uprooted trees and bushes.*

up·root·ed *verb.* Past tense of **uproot**.

Vv

valid   Correct based on facts or proof. *My experiment proved that my theory was valid.*
val·id *adjective.*

vanished   Gone from sight. *The moon vanished behind the clouds.*
van·ished *verb.* Past tense of **vanish**.

violent   Happening with or because of a strong force. *The violent earthquake destroyed many homes.*
vi·o·lent *adjective.*

Ww

warning   Notice about a danger. *The sign was a warning that the road curved sharply ahead.*
warn·ing *noun.*

water vapor   Water that is in a gaseous form and spreads throughout the atmosphere. *Water vapor began to come from the pot of boiling water on the stove.*
wa·ter va·por *noun.*

wiggled   Moved from side to side in short, sudden movements. *I wiggled my loose tooth.*
wig·gled *verb.* Past tense of **wiggle**.

Yy

young   Not old. *A joey is a young kangaroo.*
young *adjective.*

Acknowledgments

The publisher gratefully acknowledges permission to reprint the following copyrighted materials:

"Dig Wait Listen: A Desert Toad's Tale" by April Pulley Sayre, illustrated by Barbara Bash. Text copyright © 2001 by April Pulley Sayre. Illustrations copyright © 2001 by Barbara Bash. Reprinted by permission of HarperCollins Publishers.

"Farfallina and Marcel" by Holly Keller. Copyright © 2002 by Holly Keller. Reprinted with permission from Greenwillow Books, an imprint of HarperCollins Publishers.

"A Harbor Seal Pup Grows Up" by Joan Hewett and Richard Hewett. Text copyright © 2002 by Joan Hewett. Photographs copyright © 2002 by Richard Hewett. Reprinted with permission from Carolrhoda Books, Inc., a division of Lerner Publishing Group.

"Head, Body, Legs: A Story from Liberia" by Won-Ldy Paye and Margaret H. Lippert, illustrated by Julie Paschkis. Text copyright © 2002 by Won-Ldy Paye and Margaret H. Lippert. Illustrations copyright © 2002 by Julie Paschkis. Reprinted with permission from Henry Holt and Company, LLC.

"It Fell in the City" from BLACKBERRY INK by Eve Merriam. Text copyright © 1985 by Eve Merriam. Reprinted by permission of William Morrow and Company.

"Mice and Beans" by Pam Muñoz Ryan, illustrated by Joe Cepeda. Text copyright © 2001 by Pam Muñoz Ryan. Illustrations copyright © 2001 by Joe Cepeda. Reprinted by permission of Scholastic Press, a division of Scholastic Inc.

"Nutik, the Wolf Pup" by Jean Craighead George, illustrated by Ted Rand. Text copyright © 2001 by Julie Productions, Inc. Illustrations copyright © 2001 by Ted Rand. Reprinted with permission from HarperCollins Publishers.

"Officer Buckle and Gloria" by Peggy Rathmann. Text and illustrations copyright © 1995 by Peggy Rathmann. Reprinted with permission from G.P. Putnam's Sons, a division of Penguin Putnam Books for Young Readers.

"The Puppy" from RING A RING O' ROSES: FINGER PLAYS FOR PRESCHOOL CHILDREN. Reprinted with permission from Flint Public Library.

"Pushing Up The Sky" from PUSHING UP THE SKY by Joseph Bruchac. Text copyright © 2000 by Joseph Bruchac. Reprinted by permission of Penguin Putnam Books for Young Readers.

"Splish! Splash! Animal Baths" by April Pulley Sayre. Copyright © 2000 by April Pulley Sayre. Reprinted by permission of The Millbrook Press, Inc.

"Super Storms" by Seymour Simon. Text copyright © 2002 by Seymour Simon. Reprinted by permission of SeaStar Books, a division of North-South Books, Inc.

"The Tiny Seed" by Eric Carle. Copyright © 1987 by Eric Carle Corp. Reprinted with permission from Aladdin Paperbacks, an imprint of Simon & Schuster Children's Publishing Division: NY

"The Ugly Vegetables" by Grace Lin. Text and illustrations copyright © 1999 by Grace Lin. Reprinted by permission of Charlesbridge Publishing.

ILLUSTRATIONS
Cover Illustration: Luciana Navarro Powell

8–9: Diane Greenseid. 10–37: Julie Paschkis. 44–45: Diane Greenseid. 46–71: Peggy Rathmann. 74: Robert Schuster. 115: Richard Hewitt. 116–117: Jo Parry. 122–123: Bernard Adnet. 124–155: Joe Cepeda. 162–163: Pam Thompson. 164–165: Cindy Revell. 176–201: Eric Carle. 204: Daniel Del Valle. 210–233: Grace Lin. 243: Grace Lin. 254–255: Marisol Sarrazin. 256–279: Holly Keller. 281–283: Andrea Tachiera. 284: Daniel Del Valle. 290–311: Ted Rand. 310: (bc) Ted Rand, (br) Wendell Minor. 311: Ted Rand. 317–319: Daniel Del Valle. 321: Greg Harris. 332–355: Barbara Bash. 360: Jenny Vainisi. 390–391: Rex Barron. 440–441: Laura Ovreset. 442–459: Stephano Vitale. 462–463: Deborah Melmon.

PHOTOGRAPHY
All photographs are by Ken Karp for Macmillan/McGraw-Hill (MMH) except as noted below.

iv: A. Ramey/PhotoEdit. v: (tl) Jupiter Images/Comstock; (cl) Richard Hewett. vi: R. Ian Lloyd/Masterfile. vii: Maria Stenzel & Mark O. Thiessen/National Geographic Stock. viii: (tl) Glow Images/Alamy; (bl) Courtesy Peter Arnold, Inc. ix: (tl) Barbara Stitzer/PhotoEdit; (cl) Keith Kent/Science Photo Library/Photo Researchers. 2–3: A. Ramey/PhotoEdit. 4–5: (l) Geostock/Getty Images; (2) Getty Images/Blend Images. 4: (b) Mark Karrass/Corbis. 5: (br) Editorial Image, LLC/Alamy. 6–7: Corbis/PunchStock. 36: (t) Courtesy Won-Ldy Paye; (b) Courtesy of Julie Paschkis. All rights reserved. Used with permission. 38–39: Comstock/PunchStock. 40: Tom Grill/Corbis. 41: Larry Bones/AGEfotostock. 42–43: Jack Sauer/AP Images. 70: Courtesy Peggy Rathmann. 72: Kathy McLaughlin/The Image Works. 73: (t) Geri Engberg/The Image Works; (others) Richard Hutchings/PhotoEdit. 74: Photodisc Green/Getty Images. 75: Michael Newman/PhotoEdit. 76: David Nagel/Allsport Concepts/Getty Images. 77: (t) Alaska Stock LLC/Alamy; (c) Ablestock/Hemera Technologies/Alamy. 78–79: Jupiter Images/Comstock. 80: (t) Keith Brofsky/Photodisc/Getty Images; (b) Suzanne Dunn/The Image Works. 81: Pete Saloutos/Corbis. 82: Ryan McVay/Photodisc/Getty Images. 83–85: Adamsmith/Taxi/Getty Images. 86: Corbis. 88: Ryan McVay/Photodisc/Getty Images. 89: (bkgd) Bet Noire/ShutterStock; (r) C Squared Studios/Getty Images; (l) Ryan McVay/Getty Images. 90–91: Texas Parks & Wildlife Department/AP Images. 92: Tony Savino/The Image Works. 94–115: Richard Hewett. 114: (tl) Courtesy Joan Hewett. 118: Lori Adamski-Peek/Jupiter Images. 119: Larime Photo/Dembinsky Photo Associates. 120–121: Aflo Foto Agency/Alamy. 154–155: (bkgd) Wetzel & Company. 154: (t) Susan Werner. 156–157: (b) Masterfile. 158: (tl) Simon Smith/DK Images; (tc) Rachel Epstein/PhotoEdit; (tr) Andy Crawford/DK Images; (b) Jose Luis Pelaez, Inc./Corbis. 160: Rubberball/Alamy. 161: Rachel Epstein/PhotoEdit. 168–169: R. Ian Lloyd/Masterfile. 170–171: (bkgd) Brand X Pictures/PunchStock. 170: (b) David C Tomlinson/Getty Images. 171: (b) Courtesy Ned Fritz. 172–173: (c) Wolfgang Kaehler/Alamy. 174: Masterfile Royalty-Free. 175: Douglas Peebles/Corbis. 200: John Dolan. 202, 203: Macmillan McGraw-Hill. 204: Laura Dwight/PhotoEdit. 205: C Squared Studios/Photodisc Green/Getty Images. 206–207: Blend Images/PunchStock. 208–209: (b) David Young-Wolff/PhotoEdit. 208: (t) John A. Rizzo/Getty Images. 209: (c) Jose Luis Pelaez, Inc./Corbis. 232: Courtesy Grace Lin. 234–235: Panoramic Images/Getty Images. 236: (bl) Michael Newman/PhotoEdit; (bkgd) Panoramic Images/Getty Images. 237, 238: Masterfile. 239: (tl) Picture Arts/Corbis; (tc) Royalty-Free/Corbis. 240–241: Maria Stenzel & Mark O. Thiessen/National Geographic Stock. 242: Norbert Wu. 243: Marcos Brindicci/Reuters. 245: (bl) Edward Degginger/Bruce Coleman Inc.; (br) Millard H. Sharp/Photo Researchers. 246: Mike Hettwer. 247: Will Burgess/Reuters. 248: Courtesy David Krause/Madagascar Ankizy Fund. 250: Ross Whitaker/The Image Bank/Getty Images. 251: (l) Ryan McVay/Getty Images; (br) C Squared Studios/Getty Images; (tr) PhotoLink/Getty Images; (bkgd) Bet Noire/ShutterStock. 252–253: Martin Harvey/Gallo Images/Corbis. 278: Courtesy Holly Keller. 280: Frank Greenway/DK Images. 281: Stephen Dalton/NHPA. 284: Michael Newman/PhotoEdit. 285: Patricia Doyle/Getty Images. 286–287: Jeffrey L. Rotman/Getty Images. 288–289: (bkgd) Charlie Munsey/Corbis. 288: (b) Bryan & Cherry Alexander Photography/Alamy. 289: (t) Robert van der Hilst/Corbis. 310: (t) Courtesy Jean Craighead George; (b) Courtesy Ted Rand. 312–313: (bkgd) Art Wolfe/Stone/Getty Images. 313: (t) David A. Northcott/Corbis. 314: Jeff Lepore/Photo Researchers. 315: Tom Brakefield/Corbis. 316: Richard Hutchings/PhotoEdit. 320–321: (b) John Pontier/Earth Scenes. 320: (c) Scott Camazine/Photo Researchers. 321: (t) Daemon Becker. 324–325: Glow Images/Alamy. 326–327: (bkgd) Maureen Perez/iStockphoto. 326: (b) F. Lukasseck/Masterfile. 327: (br) Bob Daemmrich/Corbis. 328–329: Theo Allofs/Corbis. 330–331: (t) Norbert Rosing/National Geographic/Getty Images. 330: (b) Vince Streano/Corbis. 331: (tr) Ariel Skelley/Corbis. 354: (t) Courtesy April Pulley Sayre; (b) Courtesy Barbara Bash. 356: Stan Osolinski/Dembinsky Photo Associates. 357: (t) Joe McDonald/Corbis; (b) David Muench/Corbis. 358: George H. H. Huey/

Acknowledgments

Corbis. 359: (bl) Bill Lea/Dembinsky Photo Associates; (br) Daril Gulin/ Dembinsky Photo Associates. 360: Photodisc Green/Getty Images. 361: Beth Davidow/Getty Images. 362–363: Rolf Nussbaumer/Alamy. 364–365: (b) Lee Cates/Getty Images. 365: (t) Craig Tuttle/Corbis. 366–367: Courtesy Peter Arnold, Inc. 368–369: Peter Weimann/Animals Animals. 370–371: Ralph Reinhold/Animals Animals. 372–373: (bkgd) Tim Fitzharris/Minden Pictures. 372: (b) Gerard Lacz/Animals Animals. 374: Frans Lanting. 375: Robert Winslow/Animals Animals. 376–377: Mitch Reardon/National Audubon Society Collection/Photo Researchers. 378–379: Gunter Ziesler/Peter Arnold. 380: Frans Lanting. 381: Gregory Ochocki/National Audubon Society/Photo Researchers. 382–383: Allan Power/National Audubon Society/Photo Researchers. 384–385: Mike Severns/Getty Images. 386: Mark Phillips/National Audubon Society/ Photo Researchers. 387: Frans Lanting/Minden Pictures. 388: (tl) Frans Lanting; (tr) Courtesy April Pulley Sayre. 389: Peter Weimann/Animals Animals. 392: Ross Whitaker/The Image Bank/Getty Images. 393: Tim Davis. 394–395: Barbara Stitzer/PhotoEdit. 396: (t) Gloria H. Chomica/ Masterfile; (b) Jim Brandenburg/Minden Pictures; (inset) Judy Griesedieck. 397: ZSSD/Minden Pictures. 398–399: (b) Reed Kaestner/ Corbis. 399: (t) Walter Bibikow/The Image Bank/Getty Images; (c) Felicia Martinez/PhotoEdit; (b) Photodisc/Getty Images. 400–401: (b) Courtesy Landscape Structures Inc. 400: (t) Comstock/Alamy; (c) Karl Weatherly/Corbis; (bc) Mark Gibson/Photolibrary; (bl) Hank Morgan/ Photo Researchers. 401: (t) Arthur Tilley/Taxi/Getty Images. 402: Marko Kokic/IFRC. 404: Ryan McVay/Photodisc/Getty Images. 405: (bkgd) Bet Noire/ShutterStock; (tr) PhotoLink/Getty Images; (br) Gabe Palmer/ Alamy. 406–407: Warren Faidley/Weatherstock. 408–409: (bkgd) Ron Sanford/Corbis. 408: (b) Ellen Ozier/Reuters/Corbis. 409: (t) Mark J. Thomas/Dembinski Photo Associates. 410–411: Keith Kent/Science Photo Library/Photo Researchers. 412–413: (bkgd) George Post/Science Photo Library/Photo Researchers. 413: (c) Jim Reed/Photo Researchers. 414–415: Kent Wood/Science Source/Photo Researchers. 416–417: Kul Bhatia/ Photo Researchers. 418–419: (bkgd) NOAA Central Library, OAR/ERL/ National Severe Storms Laboratory; (c) Howard Bluestein/Photo Researchers. 420–421: (bkgd) Science VU/Visuals Unlimited. 420: (t) Nancie Battaglia/Nancie Battaglia Photography. 422–423: (bkgd) Bettmann/Corbis. 423: (t) Paul Buck/AFP/Getty Images. 426–427: (bkgd) Annie Griffiths Belt/National Geographic Stock. 426: (t) NOAA/ NESDIS/Science Source/Photo Researchers. 428–429: (bkgd) James L. Amos/Corbis. 428: (t) Joel Sartore/National Geographic Stock. 430–431: (bkgd) Howard Bluestein/Photo Researchers. 430: (t) Richard Drew/AP Images. 432–433: (bkgd) George Post/Photo Researchers. 432: (t) Courtesy Seymour Simon. 433: (c) Kent Wood/Science Source/Photo Researchers. 434–435: Bettmann/Corbis. 436: Laura Dwight/PhotoEdit. 437: Richard Hutchings/PhotoEdit. 438–439: Roger Ressmeyer/Corbis. 456: (t) Courtesy Joseph Bruchac; (b) Courtesy Stefano Vitale. 458: Courtesy Joseph Bruchac. 460: Stephen Marks/The Image Bank/Getty Images. 461: Michael Newman/PhotoEdit. 464: Richard T. Nowitz/ Corbis. 465: (t) Courtesy Tom and Anne Moore; (b) Ken Karp/ Macmillan McGraw-Hill. 468: (bl) Stone/Getty Images; (br) Peter Griffith/Masterfile. 469: (t) Mark Tomalty/Masterfile; (b) Bruce Heinemann/Getty Images. 470: Mira/Alamy. 471: (c) Digital Vision Ltd.; (b) Mark Tomalty/Masterfile. 472: Bruce Heinemann/Getty Images. 473: Jeff Greenberg/AGEfotostock. 474: (c) Paul A. Souders/Corbis; (b) David Buffington/Getty Images. 475: Peter Griffith/Masterfile. 476: Elmar Krenkel/zefa/Corbis. 477: Spencer Grant/PhotoEdit. 478: (c) Stone/Getty Images; (b) Paul Barton/Corbis. 479: Eric and David Hosking/Corbis. 480: Theo Allofs/zefa/Corbis. 481: (c) Kevin Dodge/Masterfile; (b) Brand X Pictures/Picturequest. 482: Richard Hutchings/Workbookstock. 483: Randy Faris/Corbis. 484: (t) Ian Shaw/Alamy; (b) Dale Wilson/Masterfile. 485: Martin Rugner/ AGEfotostock.

Decoding Strategy Chart

Step 1	Look for word parts (prefixes) at the beginning of the word.
Step 2	Look for word parts (suffixes) at the end of the word.
Step 3	In the base word, look for familiar spelling patterns. Think about the six syllable-spelling patterns you have learned.
Step 4	Sound out and blend together the word parts.
Step 5	Say the word parts fast. Adjust your pronunciation as needed. Ask yourself: "Is this a word I have heard before?" Then read the word in the sentence and ask: "Does it make sense in this sentence?"